Ethos

The face is of the enticing and seductive bride of the West who has adorned her countenance with ornaments and makeup, bewitching the world with her enchanting beauty. The poisonous snakes represent the locks of her hair, each of which is focused on swallowing its intended prey. That bird on the bride's head with open beaks is a crow or vulture that represents the philosophers and atheists of that region [the West] whose task is to mislead all peoples with their call to irreligiosity. At the bottom of the image are the towns and villages endowed with blessings, as well as temples and mosques and the tree [occupying the middle section of the painting], all representing the East. Faced with the witchcraft of the bride of the West and her accompanying crows and vultures and poisonous snakes, the East has wrapped the tree with honour and chastity and religion. This image was originally painted by Azim Azimzade (1880–1943), a famous caricaturist and painter, and later intellectual and cultural minister of Azerbaijan. The image was drawn exclusively for *Hophopnāmeh* of Mirza Alakbar Sabir (1862–1911), first published in 1914. The image reappeared in the 1965 Persian translation of the book and again in the 1977 edition. The later reproductions of the 1914 editions in Latinized Turkish also include the image, referred to by the title "Delber." (With special thanks to Dr. Shabnam Rahimi-Golkhandan for tracking down the image source)

Ahmad Kasravi, 'Bewitched [delbar-pendāri]', *Peymān* 2:2 (February 1935 [Bahman 1313]): 116.

Ethos

A Critique of Eurocentric Modernity

Ahmad Kasravi

Translated by Hamid Rezaei Yazdi

I.B. TAURIS
LONDON • NEW YORK • OXFORD • NEW DELHI • SYDNEY

I.B. TAURIS
Bloomsbury Publishing Plc
50 Bedford Square, London, WC1B 3DP, UK
1385 Broadway, New York, NY 10018, USA
29 Earlsfort Terrace, Dublin 2, Ireland

BLOOMSBURY, I.B. TAURIS and the I.B. Tauris logo are
trademarks of Bloomsbury Publishing Plc

First published in Great Britain 2023
This paperback edition published in 2025

Copyright © Hamid Rezaei Yazdi, 2023

Hamid Rezaei Yazdi has asserted his right under the Copyright,
Designs and Patents Act, 1988, to be identified as Editor of this work.

Series design: Adriana Brioso
Cover image: Ahmad Kasravi, 'Bewitched [delbar-pendāri]', *Peymān* 2:2 (February 1935
[Bahman 1313]): 116. Colouring by Ms. Mahtab Rafiee.

All rights reserved. No part of this publication may be reproduced or transmitted
in any form or by any means, electronic or mechanical, including photocopying,
recording, or any information storage or retrieval system, without prior
permission in writing from the publishers.

Bloomsbury Publishing Plc does not have any control over, or responsibility for,
any third-party websites referred to or in this book. All internet addresses given
in this book were correct at the time of going to press. The author and publisher
regret any inconvenience caused if addresses have changed or sites have ceased
to exist, but can accept no responsibility for any such changes.

A catalogue record for this book is available from the British Library.

A catalog record for this book is available from the Library of Congress.

ISBN: HB: 978-0-7556-4775-0
PB: 978-0-7556-4779-8
ePDF: 978-0-7556-4776-7
eBook: 978-0-7556-4777-4

Typeset by Integra Software Services Pvt. Ltd.

To find out more about our authors and books visit www.bloomsbury.com
and sign up for our newsletters.

To Ava
In whose being I learned about love

Contents

Acknowledgements ix
A note on translation x

Ahmad Kasravi's critiques of Europism and Orientalism
Mohamad Tavakoli-Targhi 1

Ethos: Book 1

1 The world and its inhabitants 19
2 Is the world progressing? 21
3 The consequence of Europe's inventions 25
4 The instruments have changed, the wars remain 29
5 Europe uproots the world's tranquillity 31
6 Can law replace religion? 35
7 Europe's woes 39
8 What will be the consequence of machinism? 45
9 What have the Prophets said and what does Europe say? 49
10 The Europist movement in Iran 53
11 The East loses its treasures 59
12 What is civilization? 63
13 European sciences 67
14 Women should not be wayward 71
15 A leader does not lie to his own people 77
16 We must refrain from looking to Europe 81
17 What is religion? 87
18 Religion is humanism 93

Ethos: Book 2

1	In God's immaculate name	101
2	How has Europe been entrapped?	105
3	Ancient grudges	109
4	Scepticism and false indoctrination	113
5	The harms of the machine	117
6	Madness	123
7	Bolshevism	127
8	Three pillars of life	133
9	Misguided guides	137
10	The ethos of coexistence	141
11	Brotherly treatment	145
12	Agricultural works	149
13	The laws of Europe [introductory remarks]	153
14	The laws of Europe [on taxation and state administration]	157
15	The laws of Europe [on jurisprudence]	161
16	Good disposition and bad disposition	167
17	The value of Europe's inventions	171
18	East and West	175
19	The Great Geneva Conventions	179
20	What is our argument?	181

Afterword
Āʿin: A defining text in Ahmad Kasravi's œuvre
Stanisław Adam Jaśkowski   186
Index   199

Acknowledgements

In completing this work, I am grateful for the encouragement and support I received from several individuals. First and foremost, credit is due to Professor Mohamad Tavakoli-Targhi whose enthusiastic encouragement first prompted this undertaking and whose brilliant introduction graces this book. Part of the production cost for this book was covered through generous funding provided by the Elahé Omidyar Mir-Djalali Institute of Iranian Studies at the University of Toronto in Canada, also made possible thanks to Professor Tavakoli-Targhi, the inaugural director of the EOM.

I also owe a debt of gratitude to the following individuals. I thank Rory Gormley, Senior Commissioning Editor at I.B.Tauris, who first saw the promise in this work back in 2017 and whose editorial vision has since contributed much to the improvement of this volume. I'm grateful to Professor Ali Mirsepassi of NYU who provided invaluable support and feedback along the way. Evan Siegel introduced me to Dr. Stanisław Jaśkowski whose original essay now appears in the Afterword. I am thankful to both of them. I am grateful for the exceptional and speedy collaboration by the wonderful editorial and production teams at I.B.Tauris (Bloomsbury) as well as the many friends and family, past and present, who read parts of the translation and provided useful feedback. I have benefited from the generous support of all these individuals, but I am alone responsible for any flaws in the finished product.

I am ultimately indebted to my family who endured the endless streaming of background music into the wee hours of the morning as I workèd and as they tried to sleep in the next room. None of this would have been possible without their loving support and understanding.

A note on translation

This book is the first complete translation in English of a treatise titled *Ā'in* by the prominent Iranian intellectual Ahmad Kasravi (1890–1946).[1] Kasravi was a polymath, reflected not only in his career as a public intellectual but also in the sheer range of topics and issues tackled in his writing: history, linguistics, contemporary politics, philosophy, literature and religion, among others. Enigmatic and polemical as Kasravi's work was, it stirred generations of intellectuals, authors, political figures and the public into reaction, whether in support or in opposition, culminating in his assassination in 1946. Given his pivotal status in the annals of Iranian intellectual history, translations of Kasravi's works into English remain surprisingly sparse.

Existing translations of Kasravi's work into English have indeed become a genre in their own right. With the possible exception of *History of the Iranian Constitutional Revolution*, the handful of other translated works foreground only a particular trajectory within Kasravi's broader vision: his denunciation of certain facets of Iranian-Islamic tradition. These include *On Islam and Shi'ism*, 'Sufism' and 'What Does Hafez Say?'[2] Another important orientation within Kasravi's thought – that is, his censure of Eurocentrism, Orientalism, and Westernization – remains limited to passing references in secondary studies but otherwise inaccessible to the English reader. The present book is an attempt to address this imbalance but also to provide unmediated access to a seminal, and consequential, work within Kasravi's œuvre.

---

[1] Apparently, this treatise was first translated into English by Mohammad Khan Khanbahador 'at the request of an American woman who had heard about *Ā'in* but could not read it because she did not know Persian'. There is, however, no indication that this translation was published. Kasravi himself had translated the first part of the book into Arabic which was reportedly published in Egypt c. 1934. Mahmud Katira'i, 'Ketāb Shenāsi-ye Kasravi' [Kasravi: A Bibliographic Survey] *Farhang-e Iran Zamin* [Encyclopedia of Iranian Culture] 18 (1971): 371–2.

[2] Works cited above, in order of appearance:

Ahmad Kasravi, *History of the Iranian Constitutional Revolution*, trans. Evan Siegel (Costa Mesa: Mazda Publishers, 2006).

Ahmad Kasravi, *On Islam and Shi'ism*, trans. M.R. Ghanoonparvar (Costa Mesa: Mazda Publishers, 1990).

Ahmad Kasravi, 'Sufism' and 'What Does Hafez Say?', in *Sufi Castigator: Ahmad Kasravi and the Iranian Mystical Tradition*, trans. Lloyd Ridgeon (London and New York: Routledge, 2006).

Kasravi's style in Persian is archaic. I have tried to preserve that style where it did not impede comprehension in English. Therefore, my translation is as literal as I could have made it in terms of diction, syntax, and vocabulary choice. This does not apply to punctuation, however, for Kasravi's text is hardly punctuated, except for end punctuation in the form of periods, question marks, exclamation marks or conjoined punctuation. The resulting text in Persian is often a string of run-on sentences that can take an entire paragraph, tagged on to each other with the conjunctive 'and'. In such cases, I have added punctuation where it may not appear in the original text. Otherwise, I have tried, as closely as typographically possible, to follow Kasravi's choice of punctuation.

Another challenge was Kasravi's coinages in Persian. This challenge had to be met with either equivalent English coinages or clarified in an explanatory footnote, or both. In either case, I have tried to convey the literal sense of the Persian coinage as much as the limits of diction allowed.

Kasravi included a limited number of footnotes in his book. I have had to add many more footnotes in order to make the text more accessible to the non-specialist reader. To differentiate the two, Kasravi's notes are indicated with typographical marks while my own notes are indicated in superscript numbers. In some cases, I have had to add a further explanatory note to the author's footnote. These are indicated with the phrase 'Translator's note' and appear in square brackets.

Āʿin was first published in 1932 and reprinted several times since. I have used the text of the third edition, published in 1978 in Tehran, as the basis for this translation.

This book follows the transliteration guidelines in Cambridge University's *Iranian Studies* journal, except in the case of anglicized words or words with commonly accepted spelling in English.

Hamid Rezaei Yazdi
Toronto, February 2022

Ahmad Kasravi's critiques of Europism and Orientalism

Mohamad Tavakoli-Targhi

Introduction

Ahmad Kasravi (b. 1890) was a prominent Iranian journalist, linguist, historian, lawyer, religious reformer and a forerunner of postcolonial criticism who was assassinated by the Devotees of Islam in 1946. As a protean political figure and prolific essayist, he embodied diverse and conflicting intellectual tendencies that fully developed in the decades after his assassination. He promoted religious homogeneity and an Islam-based polity but was critical of Shi'ism and clerical hierocracy in Iran. He was an advocate of language reform but was highly critical of Persian canonical texts. He served as a defence lawyer for the founders of the Communist Tudeh Party but was a fervent antagonist of materialism and communism. As a former seminarian, Kasravi was alarmed by the Iranian adoration of Europe, a phenomenon that he called Europism (*urupāgarā'i*). Building upon an earlier critical tradition in Persian, he viewed the Iranian mimicry of modern European norms as an 'illness' and a 'trap' (*dām*) that instead of promoting civilization and humanism would contribute to war and to social devastation. As illustrated in Hamid Rezaei Yazdi's brilliant translation of *Ethos* (*Ā'in*), Kasravi considered the idea of 'European superiority' as a deceptive device for the promotion of colonialism and capitalism. Except for scientific innovations, he explained that Iranians could improve their own modes of life and legal and administrative structures without needing to import unsuitable European norms – norms that had promoted individual greed, social inequality and world wars. He meticulously explored the mixed legacy of Orientalism, both as a purveyor of textual scholarship and as a body of knowledge in the service of European colonialism and imperialism. While appreciating the text-editing skill of Iranian literati who were influenced by Orientalists, he was highly critical of their lack of intellectual independence in the forming of Persian literary canon.

By offering a systematic critique of Europism (*urupāgarā'i*) and Orientalism, Kasravi provided the epistemological foundation for a vernacular national and religious modernity in Iran. His critiques on Europism and Orientalism shaped the works of Ahmad Fardid (1909–94), Fakhroddin Shadman (1907–67), Jalal Al-e Ahmad (1923–69), Ali Shari'ati (1933–77) and Islamic strategists such as Gholamreza Sa'edi, Ja'far Shahidi, 'Ata Allah Shahabpur and Mahdi Bazargan (1907–95). More significantly his critique of Europism bolstered the self-confidence of Iranian clerics who under his influence began to develop the outlines of a future-oriented Islamic polity. But assassinated by the Devotees of Islam in 1946 for his rationalist critique of Shi'i expectationalism and Sufi predestinarianism, Kasravi's contribution to the rationalization and futurist reorientation of religious thinking in Iran has remained unrecognized. Physically eliminated by the Devotees of Islam in 1946, Kasravi's clerical nemeses expropriated his rationalist critique of Shi'ism and Sufi predestenarianism. Fearful of clerical reprisal, the secular beneficiaries of his intellectual legacy consciously distanced themselves from him and thus contributed to his intellectual elimination. Since the Islamic Revolution of 1979, this conscious intellectual repression has been institutionalized by the prevalence of narratives that constituted the 1960s as the genesis of an authentic religious revolution in Iran. This wilful and selective amnesia has been bolstered by the works of social scientists who, by truncating the intellectual and cultural history of modern Iran, have established Jalal Al-e Ahmad, Ali Shari'ati, Ruhollah Khomeini (1902–89), Morteza Motahari (1919–79) and Mahmud Taleqani (1911–79) as the originators of a nativist and revivalist movement in Iran. But the ideas attributed to these individuals had hybrid origins, which came together in the works of Kasravi who was one of the most audacious and influential Iranian intellectuals of the twentieth century.

In his general outlook, Kasravi was influenced by a post-constitutional intellectual trend that was best exemplified by the Berlin-based journal *Iranshahr* and its editor, Hossein Kazemzadeh (1884–1962). Published between

1922 and 1927, *Iranshahr*, which was widely disseminated in Iran, included essays by Rezazadeh Shafaq, Morteza Moshfeq Kazemi (1902–77), Habib Allah Pur-e Reza and Muhammad Qazvini (1876–1949). This generation of Iranian intellectuals had developed a critical approach to European civilization and sought to articulate a vernacular modernity, a modernity that was grounded in the spiritual and ethical rejuvenation of Iran and Islam. For instance, in 1924, Moshfeq Kazemi, the editor of *Farangistan*, proposed that Iran needed a 'clerical modernity' (*tajaddod-e ākhund*).[1] A year later, Habib Allah Pur-e Reza argued that Iran was in need of a 'sacred revolution' (*enqelāb-e moqaddas*) with 'thinkers like Luther and Calvin'. Pur-e Reza believed that this sacred Revolution had to begin and end with the shedding of the blood of the clerics. In 1926, Tuti Maraghehi, addressing the Europe-travelled educated Iranian youth (*javānhā-ye tahsil kardeh va Urupā dideh*) who were 'enamoured with the outward manifestations of Europe' [*shifteh-ye jelvehā-ye zāheri-ye Urupā shodeh*], argued that 'no nation had ever reached the destiny of progress and advancement with a borrowed civilization [*tamaddon-e 'āriyeh'i*]'.[2] He argued that a borrowed civilization is like 'a borrowed attire [qabā] and shirt which are either too wide or too tight; too long or too short'.[3] He argued that educated Iranians instead of imitating Europe and 'prostrating [themselves] to the rotted skeletons of Voltaire and his likes and demanding a bloody revolution' (*beh ostokhānhā-ye pusideh-ye voltair va amsālash sojdeh kardeh enqelāb-e khunin khāsteh*), they should try to develop a distinctive Iranian civilization. Admonishing the likes of Pur-e Reza, Tuti remarked, 'it has been three thousand years now ... that we Iranians have been killing each other; is not this enough and are we still starving for bloodshed?'[4] He explained that if the 'Europe-mannered' (*urupā-ma'ābān*) Iranians seek to kill all clerics and clerics seek to kill all Europe-educated Iranians, then none will remain.[5]

---

[1] Morteza Moshfeq Kazemi, 'Zendegāni-ye Urupā'i va Zendegāni-ye Irani', *Iranshahr* 2, no. 8 (April 1924/Ordibehesht 1303): 458–67, quote on 462.

[2] Mirza Hossein Tuti Maraghehi, 'Din yā Asās-e "Elm va Tamaddon"', *Iranshahr* 4, no. 6 (August 1926/Shahrivar 1305): 347–55, quote on 352.

[3] Mirza Hossein Tuti Maraghehi, 'Din yā Asās-e "Elm va Tamaddon"', *Iranshahr*, 4, no. 6 (August 1926/Shahrivar 1305): 347–55, quote on 352.

[4] Mirza Hossein Tuti Maraghehi, 'Din yā Asās-e "Elm va Tamaddon"', *Iranshahr*, 4, no. 6 (August 1926/Shahrivar 1305): 347–55, quote on 353.

[5] Mirza Hossein Tuti Maraghehi, 'Din yā Asās-e "Elm va Tamaddon"', *Iranshahr* 4, no. 6 (August 1926/Shahrivar 1305): 347–55, quote on 353.

Like his colleagues, Kazemzadeh also believed that Iran needed an 'intellectual and religious revolution' (*enqelāb-e fekri va dini*). He explained that a religious revolution was more important than political and literary revolutions. Like Ahmad Kasravi, Kazemzadeh defined religion as 'ideas, beliefs, habits, and ethics that have been recognized as religion in Iran'. He believed that a large majority of Iranians were intellectually, spiritually and physically influenced by religion and thus 'the rein of their reason, thinking, and national sensibilities [*zamām-e 'uqul va afkār va hasāsiyat-e mellat*] were in the hands of the clerics and the religious teachers'.[6] For Kazemzadeh, this revolution involved 'the purging of superstitions and superfluities [*khurāfāt va ezāfāt*]' from Shi'ism. This call for purging was important since in accordance with 'true meaning of religion' (*ma'nā-ye haqiqi-ye din*) 'there would be no irreligious individuals anywhere in the world but in Iran (*joz Iran*)'.[7] Again similar to Kasravi, Kazemzadeh expounded that 'by religious revolution I neither intend the establishment of a new religion nor the encouragement of irreligiously' but instead 'the explication of the truth and the essence of religion and its concordance [*tatbiq*] with modern civilization'.[8] Kazemzadeh, who had called for the establishment of 'Occidentology' (*gharb shenāsi*) as a field of inquiry in Iran, argued that the 'material progress of the West' (*taraqiyāt-e māddi-ye gharb*) should be synthesized with the 'spirituality of the East' (*ma'naviyāt-e sharq*). He prescribed a 'blended modernity' that sought the concordance of 'science with religion, materiality with spirituality, life with endeavour, and endeavour with virtue'.[9] In this scenario 'a modern person must be religious and a religious person must be modern'.[10] Such prevailing views in the 1920s provide the pertinent context for a historically situated understanding of Ahmad Kasravi's critique of Europism and his detraditionalization of Islam, a futurist project that antagonized the Iranian guardians of Islamic tradition in Iran.

---

[6] Kazemzadeh, 'Din va Melliyat', *Iranshahr* 3, no. 1/2 (Day 1293): 1–44; quoted 1–2.
[7] Kazemzadeh, 'Din va Melliyat', *Iranshahr* 3, no. 1/2 (Day 1293): 1–44; quote on 2.
[8] Kazemzadeh, 'Din va Melliyat', *Iranshahr* 3, no. 1/2 (Day 1293): 1–44; quote on 5.
[9] Kazemzadeh, Hossein, *Rahbar-e Nezhād-e Naw*, Berlin: *Iranshahr* Press, 1928, 4.
[10] Kazemzadeh, *Rahbar-e Nezhād-e Naw*, 4.

Europism

Published in 1932, 'Ethos' (*Ā'in*) is a foundational work of Ahmad Kasravi the themes of which resonate in all his social, cultural, literary, religious and political essays. A forerunner of postcolonial criticism, Kasravi's *Ā'in* offered a comprehensive critique of European civilization and the mimetic project of Europism (*urupāgarā'i*), a futurist project that viewed the present of the West as the future of the Rest. At the distinct conjecture of the early 1930s, it discerned that European innovations, despite their attractive appearance, promoted war, destruction, hunger and unemployment, and were thus leading to a 'malicious destiny' ('*āqebat-e shum*).[11] Chastising the Iranian Europhiles for their lack of intellectual independence, it called for an alternative path of progress and development that could avoid the social and economic problems of Europe. All along, Kasravi was keenly aware of the discursive construction of the East and the West arguing that this division was initially introduced by Europeans. Arguing against geographic essentialism, he explained:

> 'We are not claiming that the people of the East and West are different or that Europeans are innately ignoble [*nāsotudeh*]. Never! Europe was also similar to the East until in the past few centuries it attained certain inventions – inventions which it applauds and boasts of. But the truth is that these innovations are the cause of the world's destruction'.

Kasravi dismissed the notion of European superiority that predicated the call for a wholesale Europeanization of Iran. He recalled, 'Europe boasts that its innovations in the past two to three centuries have contributed to the well-being and the advancement of the world and it considers each modern innovation as an additional step toward progress and superiority'.[12] To evaluate this pretension, like Kazemzadeh, Kasravi scrutinized the 'destiny' (*maqsad*) that was embedded in the concept of 'progress' (*pishraft*). He explained that both Europeans and non-Europeans conceive human 'welfare and happiness' (*āsāyesh va khorsandi*) as their universal and all-inclusive goals.[13] Having discerned this common destiny, he argued that 'besides some praiseworthy

---

[11] Kasravi, Ahmad. *Ā'in*, 3rd ed. Tehran, Roshdiyyeh, 1978, 4.
[12] Kasravi, *Ā'in*, 5.
[13] Kasravi, *Ā'in*, 5.

medical discoveries, other European innovations are not worthy of boasting about and raising one's neck in glory [over them]'.[14] While 'master of tool-making' (*abzār sāzi*), Europe had failed in promoting human welfare and happiness.[15] He rhetorically asked whether European inventions have reduced the work-time, made food more plentiful and prolonged human life.[16] Resentful of military technology, which he considered as 'the machinery of homicide', Kasravi argued that these machines 'promoted the vending of bloodshed and murder [*bāzār-e khunrizi va jānsetāni*] and multiplied injuries and destruction'.[17]

For Kasravi the public image of Europe did not correspond to its post-war realities. With the European slogan of 'strive, strive' (bekush, bekush), most Easterners believed that Europe was 'heaven on earth and that its population lived in happiness and joy'. He reported,

> Easterners everywhere have risen and hurriedly try to make their own countries like Europe. They institute European laws and promote European habits and morality amongst their families. Men and women proudly fashion [*ārāyesh*] themselves in European style. The sole desire of every nation is to catch up with Europe prior to others so that, as it is claimed, they can reach the caravan of civilization. But they are all so disoriented that they trample on religion, piety, and morality, which are the most valuable treasures of the East.[18]

Like Kazemzadeh, Kasravi attributed this adoration of Europe to European colonial ventures and to the dispatching of travellers to the East, both of which he considered as responses to the crisis of over-production and the search for new markets.

These European efforts were bolstered by the emergence of movements for 'the acquiring of freedom or Europism [*urupāgarā'i*]' in the East.[19] During the Iranian Constitutional Revolution, for instance, 'the demand for justice' ('*edālat khāhi*) precipitated into 'a desire for Europe (*urupā-khāhi*)'. After the subsiding

---

[14] Kasravi, *Ā'in*, 10.
[15] Kasravi, *Ā'in*, 13.
[16] Kasravi, *Ā'in*, 7.
[17] Kasravi, *Ā'in*, 10.
[18] Kasravi, *Ā'in*, 27.
[19] Kasravi, *Ā'in*, 28.

of the revolution, Kasravi explained that 'essayists and orators all over Iran claimed that the people were solely seeking Europism, and adoring Europe, they thus fabricated many lies and exaggerations'.[20] From their perspective, Kasravi sarcastically reported,

> Europe is the source of every virtue and excellence and Europeans, both men and women, are angels on Earth. Civilization, which is lacking all over the world, is an exclusive privilege of life in Europe and it must be delivered from there to other lands along with the automobile, the cinema, and the theatre. Iranians must acquire from Europe everything, including law, morality, and custom.[21]

Their conclusive view, according to Kasravi, was that 'everything European is noble and elegant and everything Eastern is ignoble and vile'. Referring to a statement that was attributed to Hasan Taqizadeh, he disapprovingly reported: 'Iranians must become European physically and spiritually, internally and externally'.[22] To discredit this mimetic call for a comprehensive Europeanization, he explained that the enthusiasts of Europe were unaware that in every corner of Europe millions were unemployed, homeless and hungry.[23]

In his examination of Europism, Kasravi observed that the most effective device for European domination was the 'ridiculing' (*rishkhand*) and the 'disparaging' (*sarkuft*) of non-European modes of life. As a result of this practice that had become prevalent among the Iranian journalists and the returnees from Europe, Kasravi believed that 'with this ploy the most rebellious person can be pacified'.[24] 'Science, civilization, superiority, and advancement' were all utilized by Europeans, in this analysis, for the purpose of 'plundering Eastern wealth' and for inducing the people to abandon their modest mode of life. As a result of Europeanization, he explained, religiosity, piety, charity, the consoling of the poor and the aiding of the deprived, modesty and other Eastern moral values subsided and 'in their place irreligiosity, impiety, selfishness, pleasure-seeking, greed, short-sightedness, and combativeness prevail among the

---

[20] Kasravi, *Āʿin*, 29.
[21] Kasravi, *Āʿin*, 29.
[22] Kasravi, *Āʿin*, 29.
[23] Kasravi, *Āʿin*, 25.
[24] Kasravi, *Āʿin*, 29.

youth'.[25] He viewed the youths who enthusiastically embraced European values as 'the disgrace of their own time' (*nang-e zamān-e khod*).[26]

Reflecting on this naive enthusiasm, Kasravi observed that 'unlike Easterners who praise everything European, Europeans belittle everything Eastern'.[27] Dismissing both the arrogance of Europeans and the naivety of Europists, he believed that 'the ancient and unglamorous East has invaluable inventories, inventories that are the foundation for the welfare of the world'.[28] He contrived that the 'wretched who have rendered their hearts to Europe' (*deldādegān-e furumāyeh-ye urupā*) are either 'mercenaries of European companies or hate their own land and home; otherwise [the notion of] European superiority and distinctiveness is the cheapest babble'.[29] As evidence for the absurdity of European superiority, he enumerated the hardship of workers, the arrogance of capitalists, the intensified class struggle and the millions of unemployed youths. He explained that 'in a land where life is based upon sustained efforts for the accumulation of money without regard for others, civilization is many miles away'.[30] He wondered how anyone could 'be proud of the advancement of sciences that had produced bombs, tanks, and homicidal gases'.[31] Admonishing the military utility of science in Europe, he explained that the 'sciences were beneficial and appeared as harmless as long as they had not fallen into the hands of Europeans; but contemporary science is more harmful than beneficial'.[32] Some European scientists who bear the titles of 'Professor' and 'Doctor', instead of promoting human happiness, according to Kasravi, had made science the instrument of 'thievery and deceit' (*dozdi va daghalkāri*).[33] Focusing on the destructive use of technology, he viewed it as shameful that instead of promoting kindness and philanthropy, science had promoted ignobility and defiance. Considering 'tool-making' (*abzār sāzi*) as the primary accomplishment of

---

[25] Kasravi, *Ā'in*, 31.
[26] Kasravi, *Ā'in*, 33.
[27] Kasravi, *Ā'in*, 33.
[28] Kasravi, *Ā'in*, 33.
[29] Kasravi, *Ā'in*, 34.
[30] Kasravi, *Ā'in*, 36.
[31] Kasravi, *Ā'in*, 37.
[32] Kasravi, *Ā'in*, 37.
[33] Kasravi, *Ā'in*, 39.

contemporary Europe, Kasravi considered Europeans as 'master ironworkers' (*ostād-e āhangari*) whose philosophical views could be dismissed as 'the most meaningless prattle' (*bihudeh-tarin sokhan*).[34]

Evaluating the 'detriments of the machine' (*āsibhā-ye māshin*), Kasravi observed that while reducing 'hand-toils' (*ranj-e dasthā*) by one hundredth, the machine had intensified heart-toils (*ranj-e delhā*) by a thousand fold. Critical of the contribution of mechanization to the intensification of social inequalities, he recalled how millions had become unemployed and suffered from hunger in America, England, Germany, and Poland. Thus, he rhetorically asked, 'Are not these shameful for the world? … Is this the meaning of welfare [*āsudegi*] promised by the machine?'[35] He asked, 'what is the value of this hellish tool when the world is suffering from it so much?'[36] In his ethical criticism of 'the hellish machinery' (*abzār-e duzakhi*), Kasravi argued that 'the machine must work for humans and not humans for the machine'. He attributed this assumed reversal to the insanity of Europeans.[37] Blaming mechanization for the rampant social problems in Europe and the United States, he argued that such problems did not exist in countries that had not over-mechanized. To encounter the problems of the Great Depression, he called for demechanization.[38]

Kasravi sought to dissuade people from pursuing Europe's 'dangerous and injurious path' (*rāh-e bimnāk va por āsib*).[39] He believed that despite the growth of Europism, Eastern nations had not yet become entangled in European problems and 'could return from the mid-way and erect a wall between [themselves] and the West and peacefully attend to [their] own affairs'.[40] Kasravi's audacious encounter with Iranian Europists was guided by the retrospection that the modern European ethos had made daily life more strenuous and 'as our life has become more laborious, we have proportionally regressed'.[41]

---

[34] Kasravi, *Āʿin*, respectively, 40 and 39.
[35] Kasravi, *Āʿin*, 2:15.
[36] Kasravi, *Āʿin*, 2:18.
[37] Kasravi, *Āʿin*, 2:19.
[38] Kasravi, *Āʿin*, 2:17.
[39] Kasravi, *Āʿin*, 49.
[40] Kasravi, *Āʿin*, 49.
[41] Kasravi, *Āʿin*, 50.

Critiquing Orientalism

Kasravi's critique of Orientalism was a corollary of his reprobation of Europe and Europism. His evaluation was informed by an earlier critical tradition in Persian coupled with his own personal interactions with contemporary Orientalists and their Iranian disciples. In a 1933 essay, 'East and West' (*Sharq va Gharb*),[42] he identified Orientalism as 'one of the wonders of our time' (*shegeftihā-ye zamān-e mā*). 'Our history, language and literature,' he remarked emphatically, 'are being edited [*tadvin*] by foreigners [thousands] of miles away from us.'[43] Reflecting on the emergence of Orientalism, he explained:

> It is evident that Orientalism was a product of Europeans eyeing up the countries of the East. To dominate the Easterners with informed conduct and behaviour, they found it necessary to study the religions and languages of the peoples of the East and to gain knowledge about their history, nature, and characteristics. This explains the emergence of Orientalism as an institution with both benefits and costs for the people of the East. On one hand [Orientalists] investigated language, history, and similar fields and acquired valuable knowledge, which was also beneficial to Easterners. On the other hand, they utilized this knowledge for deceiving and misleading the Easterners.[44]

While respectful of an older generation of scholars like James Dadmesteter (1849–94), Theodore Nöldke (1836–1930), Ferdinand Justi (1837–1907), Josef Markwart (1864–1930), Vasily Barltold (1869–1930), George Rawlinson (1812–1902), Fredrich Carl Andreas (1846–1930) and Arthur Emanuel Christensen (1875–1945), Kasravi was critical of his contemporary Iranologists who were accused of turning the field into a wealth-accumulating and swindling (*māl-anduzi va kolāh bardāri*) enterprise.[45] Finding their works inadequate and un-rigorous, he argued that it would be just as well if 'their headless and taleless babbles' (*sokhanān-e bisar va tah*) were pounded on their heads. He was

---

[42] Kasravi, 'Sharq va Gharb,' *Armaghan* (Ordibehesht 1312).
[43] Ahmad Kasravi, 'Sharq va Gharb', *Armaghan* 14: 2 (Ordibehesht 1312); reprinted in *Kārvand-e Kasravi*, ed. Yahya Zoka (Tehran: Ketabhā-ye Jibi, 1352), 411–14; quote on 411.
[44] Kasravi, 'Pas cherā kasāni az shāerān havādāri minamāyand,' *Dar Pirāmun-e Adabiyāt*, 146–7.
[45] Ahmad Kasravi, 'Sharq va Gharb', *Armaghan* 14: 2 (Ordibehesht 1312); reprinted in *Kārvand-e Kasravi*, ed. Yahya Zoka (Tehran: Ketabhā-ye Jibi, 1352), 411–14; quote on 411.

particularly critical of those who relied on the research works of native scholars but failed to cite them in their own derivative publications. For instance, he complained that his own original research on Azeri language was appropriated by an author of the *Encyclopedia of Islam*. Addressing the author, he asked: 'why is there no mention of my essay? Is it fair that ... you mention Professor Browne because he had edited *Silsilat al-Nasab*[-e Safaviyyeh] (*Genealogy of the Safavid Dynasty*), but you fail to mention me and my books from which you had obtained the information?'[46] Kasravi explained that what really bothered him was the Orientalists' differential treatment of Asians and Europeans.[47]

Kasravi's most controversial attack on Orientalism was part of a heated debate on literature and poetry that was initiated in 1935/1314. In 'What is Hafiz Saying?' (*Hafez Cheh Miguyad?*) he argued that Orientalists who adored Hafez (d. 1390) and Sa'di (b. 1210) 'had evil-intentions for the East'. He found it duplicitous that Europeans 'produced variegated machinery of warfare and trained their youth as soldiers, pilots, and parachuters', but suspiciously preferred Easterners like Hafez, Khayyam and Sa'di who wasted their time on word-playing and rhyme-minting.[48] By praising such poets who promoted 'fatalism' and 'indolence', Kasravi believed that Orientalists were more effective than millions of soldiers in disempowering the people.[49] At a juncture when the classical texts of Persian literature were actively edited and printed, he initiated a spirited attack against Persian scholars like Muhammad 'Ali Furughi (1877–1942) and Isa Seddiq (1894–1978) who, in his view, were mindlessly imitating the Orientalist canonization of the Persian literature. Kasravi explained that scholars like Furughi and Seddiq naively believed that the best way to represent Iran to the world would be through the works of the classical poets who were well known in Europe.[50] Dismissing such a view as simplistic, he alleged that European praises were intended 'to deceive the poor people of the East'.[51] He believed that both

---

[46] Ahmad Kasravi, 'Sharq va Gharb', *Armaghan* 14: 2 (Ordibehesht 1312); reprinted in *Kārvand-e Kasravi*, ed. Yahya Zuka (Tehran: Ketabha-ye Jibi, 1352), 411–14; quote on 414.
[47] Ahmad Kasravi, 'Sharq va Gharb', *Armaghan* 14: 2 (Ordibehesht 1312); reprinted in *Kārvand-e Kasravi*, ed. Yahya Zoka (Tehran: Ketabhā-ye Jibi, 1352), 411–14; quote on 414.
[48] Kasravi, Ahmad. *Hafez Cheh Miguyad*. Tehran: Peyman, 1943, 30.
[49] Kasravi, *Hafez Cheh Miguyad*, 30.
[50] Kasravi Ahmad. *Dar Pirāmun-e Adabiyāt*. Tehran: Bāhamād-e Āzādegān, 1947, 19.
[51] Kasravi 'ziyān-e bas bozorgi keh az sh'erhā barkhāsteh,' in *Dar Pirāmun-e Adabiyāt*, 63.

the Orientalists and their Iranian disciples were inducing 'indolence' and 'fatalism' by recirculating poetic texts belonging to a 'morally degenerated' period of Iranian history. Thus, almost fifty years prior to Edward Said, he censured the Iranian disciples of British Orientalists for contributing to their own self-Orientalization. Resorting to a conspiratorial view, he asserted that the British sought to nullify the ideals of the Constitutional Revolution by publicizing a poetry and literature that encouraged predestinarianism and deterred social activism.⁵² He alleged that Orientalists like Edward G. Browne (1862–1926) were 'aware of the temperament of contemporary Iranians and the weakness of their spirit. They knew well that with a song in Europe thousands would rock [in Iran]'.⁵³

While a keen critic, Kasravi clearly failed to discern the complex reciprocal relations of Orientalists with their Iranian associates. This was most evident in Browne's works, which bear the traces of his cooperation with Ahmad Ruhi, Mirza Aqa Khan Kermani, Muhammad Qazvini, Hossein Kazemzadeh and Hasan Taqizadeh, among others. For instance, citing the introduction to *Noqāt al-Kāf*, which was published under the name of Browne, conspiratorial theorists often viewed this as a convincing document of British support for the Babi movement. Contrary to these assertions, it is now well-established that this controversial introduction was written by Muhammad Qazvini who had asked Browne to accept its authorship.⁵⁴ Thus, Iranian associates of Orientalists were active and crafty partners in the development of a scholarly tradition that has been often viewed as an exclusively European enterprise.

Despite his conspiratorial lapses, Kasravi was a firm believer in the Enlightenment motto of 'Dare to Think' (*Supra Aude*) as expressed by Immanuel Kant. In endeavours against the Iranian literati, he insisted that it was not significant what Goethe (1749–1832) or Fitzgerald had said about Hafez or Khayyam. Instead of mimicking European literary judgments, he advocated that Iranians should independently assess their own literary tradition and canonize only works that encouraged human agency and promoted human welfare and happiness.

---

⁵² Kasravi, *Dar Pirāmun-e Adabiyāt*, 18–19.
⁵³ Kasravi, 'Pas cherā kasāni az shāʻerān havādāri minamāyand,' *Dar Pirāmun-e Adabiyāt*, 146–152.
⁵⁴ For instance, see Golpayigani.

Islamism as counter-Europism

Kasravi's appraisal of Europe led him to the moral injunction to '[take] eyes off Europe'. Believing that 'Europe faced a very fearful future', he called for the purging of the 'malady of Europism' (*dard-i urupāgarā'i*) and returning to the noble values that were trampled upon by Europists.⁵⁵ In his counter-Europist future, 'religion' (*din*) played a pivotal role. But it is significant to recall that Kasravi's definition of 'religion', like that of Kazemzadeh, resembled the use of 'ideology' in his contemporary Europe. He viewed religion as humanism (*ādamigari*)⁵⁶ and as 'the source of worldly prosperity' (*māyeh-ye ābādāni-ye jahān*).⁵⁷ Essential to this unfamiliar worldly definition was an 'inclination toward human ethos' (*beh ā'in-e ādami garāyand*)⁵⁸ and the promotion of 'public welfare' (*āsāyesh-e hamegān*).⁵⁹ As a paradigm of ethical life, Kasravi's Islam was a rational and future-looking project rather than a sedimented tradition grounded in fatalism and expectationalism. To re-establish Islam as a 'guide for life' (*dastur-e zendegi*), he called for the returning of Islam to its foundation (*mā mibāyest Islam rā beh bonyād-e khod bargardānim*),⁶⁰ which in his assessment consisted of an orderly world and a future-bound rational life.⁶¹ The promotion of a scientific, rational and futural Islam was one of the major tasks that Kasravi set for himself and his disciples, a task that prompted a radical rethinking of Islam but antagonized the guardians of Shi'i eschatology.

With his intensifying anti-clericalism and ambiguous and often misunderstood neologisms, Kasravi became the target of sustained and unrelenting attack. His book-burning ceremonies provided the basis for the unsubstantiated accusation that in these gatherings he burned the *Qur'an*. With his attack against the literati and their celebration of Hafez, Sa'di and Khayyam, Furughi and Dashti accused him of claiming to be a new prophet. To fight against their common enemy, thus the guardians of Shi'i tradition joined hands with the self-proclaimed guardians of Persian literary tradition.

---

[55] Kasravi, *Ā'in*, 47, 48.
[56] Kasravi, *Ā'in*, 56.
[57] Kasravi, *Ā'in*, 52.
[58] Kasravi, *Ā'in*, 57.
[59] Kasravi, *Ā'in*, 57.
[60] Kasravi, Ahmad. *Mā Cheh Mikhāhim*. Tehran: Peyman, 1941, 200.
[61] Kasravi, *Mā Cheh Mikhāhim*, 200.

With the fall of Reza Shah in 1941 and the revival of clerical activism, the anti-Kasravi campaign became a primary purpose of the newly emerging religious organizations. For instance the celebrated Muhammad Taqi Shari'ati was a key anti-Kasravi activist in Mashhad and these activities constituted the pre-history of his Centre for the Dissemination of Islamic Truths (*Kānun-e Nashr-e Haqāyeq-e Eslāmi*).[62]

But anti-Kasravi actions and publicity contributed to his increasing militancy and what became an all-out struggle against the clerical establishment. Having become the target of sustained verbal and physical abuses, Kasravi argued that 'Constitutional life and the Shi'i sect are very discordant' [*zendegāni-ye mashruteh bā kish-e Shi'i besyār nāsāzgār ast*].[63] Anticipating the present-day constitutional debates over 'representative or custodial' [*vekālat* or *velāyat*] government in the Islamic Republic, Kasravi argued that in a constitutional government sovereignty is the people's right ... whereas in Shi'ism sovereignty is the right of the ulama.[64] He argued that Shaykh Fazl Allah Nuri who was executed in 1909 as a counter-revolutionary was correct in his assertion that 'Constitutionalism is contrary to Shi'ism'.[65] Kasravi explained that the Shi'i denomination 'cannot and would not resonate with democracy'. He firmly believed the status of the clerics in the post-Reza Shah period had created a 'great dilemma' (*gereftāri-ye bozorg*) that contributed to 'the ill-fate of Iran'. He warned that 'the shah, the Parliament, and the government should not view this as a simple matter and remain indifferent to the danger that they pose'. As a champion of rational public discourse, Kasravi called upon the prime minister Morteza Qoli Bayat (1890–1958) to organize a public debate where these constitutional issues could be debated between himself and the ulama.[66] But during this period of reconciliation between the government and the Shi'i clerics, Kasravi's call for public debate fell on deaf ears. Instead of debating, his opponents planned to assassinate him, a plan that was executed during a court hearing on 11 March 1946.

---

[62] Sadr al-Sadat, 'Do nemuneh fadākāri,' *Parcham-e Islam*, 63 (25 Tir 1326), 3.
[63] Kasravi, Ahmad. *Dowlat beh Mā Pāsokh Dahad*. Tehran: Peyman, 1945, 12.
[64] Kasravi, *Dowlat beh Mā Pāsokh Dahad*, 13.
[65] Kasravi, *Dowlat beh Mā Pāsokh Dahad*, 13.
[66] Kasravi, *Dowlat beh Mā Pāsokh Dahad*, 24.

With Kasravi's assassination, his call for the rationalization of religious thinking was coopted by Islamist strategists like Gholamreza Sa'edi, Ja'far Shahidi, Muhammad Nakhshab, Muhammad Taqi Shari'ati and Islamist journals like *Parcham-e Islam, Donyā-ye Islam* and *Maktab-e Islam*. Kasravi's critique of Europism was continued by Rahimzadeh Safavi,[67] Rezazadeh Shafaq, Ahmad Fardid, Fakhroddin Shadman, Jalal Al-e Ahmad and 'Ali Shari'ati. His critique of Orientalism was also elaborated by Daryush Ashuri, Ehsan Naraqi and Hamid Enayat, among others. While Kasravi's ideas gained public currency in the 1960s and the 1970s, the beneficiary of his ideas consciously elided all references to him for fear of antagonizing the clerics.

Kasravi's self-confident critique of Europism and Orientalism provided the foundations for a vernacular modernity that instead of resisting social change advocated a futurist Islamic social and political order. The futurist Islam advanced by the Iranian Islamists since the 1940s was informed by Kasravi's denunciation of Shi'i millenarianism and Sufi predestinarianism. Believing in a progressive divine plan that unfolds through human agency, Kasravi explained that Shi'i eschatology was an alien innovation that had nothing to do with 'pure Islam'. He thus argued that true Muslims, instead of waiting for God's intervention and the Mahdi's return, must work actively for the promotion of justice and progressive social transformation, a perspective that also informed Ayatollah Khomeini's notion of *vilāyat-e faqih*. As an advocate of human agency, Kasravi was critical of a fatalistic Sufi trend within Persian religious and literary traditions. This brought him into an open conflict with the ulama and with literary scholars who were canonizing Hafez, Sa'di, and Khayyam as exemplars of Persian poetic tradition. Going public with these debates, Kasravi antagonized the Shi'i ulama, the literary scholars and the Europhile politicians.

---

[67] Rahimzadeh Safavi, 'Eghrāz-e movarrekhin-e urupā'i', *Mehr* 3: 2 (Tir 1314), 143–6; idem, 'Mo'alefāt-e urupā'i, mo'alefāt-e mashreqi va ta'sir-e ānhā dar melal-e mashreq zamin', *Mehr* 3: 1 (Khordād 1314/Khordād 1315), 18–21.

Ethos: Book One

Chapter One

The world and its inhabitants

The world is [akin to] a desert and its inhabitants are caravanners in it, eternally bewildered and misguided. Many a leader rose to guide. However, their call was not heeded except by a certain group while the others still remained misguided in the desert.

Is it the destiny of humans to be eternally lost, with all their knowledge and wisdom, to not distinguish gain from loss but to mistake loss for gain and steer away daily from tranquillity and contentment?

Woe to humankind who despite being the best of creation and having the unique gift of thought and wisdom has not provided as much tranquillity and contentment for himself as dumb beasts and cannot enjoy life's blessings as much as four-legged animals!

This human who has claimed the expanse of the world at the expense of other creatures nevertheless does not live a comfortable and content life, adding every moment hardships and displeasure to his life!

Especially in our age the world's caravan has succumbed to a curious misguidance, an aberration unlike ever before! Throngs of people have taken a path whose end is annihilation; others have followed it mindless of their steps or without feeling anxious about the destination awaiting them.

The world had never witnessed such a vile state. The path Europe* has taken to life, and others whether willingly or unwillingly follow suit, this path has an ominous outcome. The world appears orderly and beautiful, but its inhabitants are deprived of tranquillity and happiness as a person who has adorned himself and donned beauteous garments but is deprived of good health which is the sole source of pleasure and happiness!

---

* Here and elsewhere in this book the term 'Europe' is intended to mean the entire West, whether Europe or America.

Europe boasts of its glamorous and opulent cities and of its countless inventions, but these same European inventions have created entanglements in the thread of human life, hopes for the untangling of which are faint, but also it is gravely feared that this thread come undone and the world be devoid of tranquillity and contentment for years even centuries, and who knows what destiny awaits those beauteous cities of Europe?!

Or who knows that the world with these automobiles, aeroplanes, railroads, electric lights, telegraph, radio, cinemas, and other such European adornments is not itself similar to the sacrificial camel, rallied merrily through the bazars and town quarters, adorned with tassels and cowbells, surrounded by buglers and horsemen riding front and rear, all the while that poor brute unawares that this embellishment and jubilation is the messenger of sudden death!!

Chapter Two

Is the world progressing?

Europe boasts that its innovations in the past two to three centuries have contributed to the well-being and advancement of the world and it considers each modern innovation as an additional step towards progress and superiority. Are this boast and this fancy justified? Has the world truly progressed in the recent two to three centuries?

First, we must determine what the world is seeking. In other words, it can be discerned from the term 'progress' that we have a destination in mind and strive to get closer to it – what is this destination?

It is cause for happiness that on this issue our aim is the same as Europe's; we all believe that the cause of goodness in the world and the sole desire of its inhabitants is tranquillity and contentment.*

This intent is the worthiest in creation. Prophets have risen, religions have been revealed, kingdoms have been established, laws have been instated all for this purpose. The wars that have been waged, the bloods that have been shed, the revolts that have erupted have all been on this pretext. All the bureaus that are functional in every city today do so in the name of that intent.

All the factions that exist with different designations in Europe today, the conferences initiated by governments, the League of Nations which has been established after Europe's global war[1] and which in Europeans' estimation is the worthiest establishment in the world, all of these are undertaken in the name of peace and contentment.

---

* That in newspapers they use the term 'happiness' [khosh bakhti] instead of contentment [khorsandi] is a mistake.
[1] Reference to the First World War (1914–18). Following the war, at the Paris Peace Conference, the League of Nations was established in January 1920 as an intergovernmental body tasked with maintaining global peace.

It is likewise indisputable that the intent is the welfare of all people, whether they be affluent or destitute, workers or employers, privileged or disadvantaged, so that every household, of any race or essence they might be, wherever they may live and in whatever state they might be, can live comfortably and feel content with their lives as much as possible, not that in every city or town only one group live in comfort and gaiety while others burn in the fire of poverty.

Let us now see whether these novel European inventions which have appeared in the last few centuries have added to humanity's tranquillity and contentment. Have the toils of humankind in life decreased through riding cars and trains, through flying with airplanes, through speaking with telephones, through sending messages by telegraph, through going to cinemas, or through listening to the radio?

Alas, no! Pity, no!

On the contrary it must be said that as a consequence of these inventions and the inevitable transformations that have appeared in life, the toils of humans have increased daily and massive throngs of humanity have never undergone the hardship and distress which they endure today.

We remember full well the extent of our tranquillity until twenty years ago when we still had our own ancient Eastern life [style] compared with the degree of our hardships now that we have been contaminated with Western life [style]. We are still at the beginning of this road and if we do not return from this path which we have taken after the Westerners, our difficulty and entanglement will be manifold.

The appropriate explanation for this remark [is] thus: two things in life cause humans distress: one [is] want of fodder and clothing and shelter and other necessities of life, the other the battle and conflict among people in the name of enmity and rivalry which is eternally afoot.

In other words, every living thing – be it human or animal – has no other option but to battle the world (nature) in order to obtain food and clothing and shelter and other necessities of life, and also battle his own kind in order to prevent them from harming him through robbery or deception or other means or stealing his belongings out of his hands or his rivals surpassing him and restricting his and his line's access to sustenance.

Everyone's life starts with these two battles and comes to end with these two battles. But we can consider battle with the world a menial task. Specially after the discoveries and inventions introduced by Europeans and their mastery over the world (nature), today this latter battle is the easiest of tasks.

Catastrophic* is the battle that humans have with each other whose severity increases day by day. If it weren't for this catastrophic battle among humans the earth would be heaven high! The root of the problem is that since the beginning of creation humans have been predisposed to be each other's rivals and enemies, each having free rein in oppressing the others. If there are a hundred afflictions in the world, only one comes from illness, impoverishment, cold and heat all of which have easy cure. The remaining ninety-nine afflictions come about through humankind's own tyranny.

So many wars have been waged in the world, so much blood shed, anarchies fermented, these are all the consequence of the struggle among humans. The movements that exist throughout the world today, the millions of armies that have been mobilized, the factionalism and enmity that have appeared among states in the East and West are all specimen of this catastrophic battle among earthlings. Prophets have risen, laws have been enacted to cure the world of this excruciating pain.

An excruciating pain that has exceedingly intensified today. If in ancient times the harm of this pain had subsided as a result of religion and the prophets' toils, during the past two to three centuries of Europe's rise, its severity has increased daily and today it has reached such a state that if we do not concern ourselves with [finding] a cure we must perforce lose hope in the betterment of the world.

If there is any benefit in European discoveries and inventions of which they boast so much, it is merely to overcome the natural world.

Those who consider these discoveries and inventions to be the source of goodness in the world have forgotten that the pain that must be healed is the hostility and conflict that humans have among themselves. Only that invention or discovery can be considered as the source of goodness in the world and can be exalted that uproots this conflict or that lessens its severity.

---

* The word 'patiyāreh' means catastrophe. [Translator's note: Kasravi uses the word 'patiyāreh' in its classical sense. He finds it necessary to clarify its meaning, however, because the contemporary usage of the term 'patiyāreh' in Persian denotes a shrew.]

Here a parable must be recalled: in a village there was hostility and sectarianism among its inhabitants which occasionally erupted in uproar in which they wounded each other's heads and faces with sticks and rocks.

A master sword maker arrived from the city and settled there, crafting swords and giving them to the villagers so that from then on when there was uproar they easily shed each other's blood and in each conflict several contenders died.

Meanwhile, the sword maker fanned the flames of conflict in order to sustain his trade until after some years a holy man arrived in the village and extinguished the fire of conflict with his sincere counsel, eradicating hostility among the villagers.

The world is [like] this village and the hostilities among humans are [like] that conflict and sectarianism [among the villagers]. And only he who obliterates conflict among peoples or lessens its severity can parade his good deeds before the world and boas of his achievement; otherwise European inventions which are in fact the tools of conflict are like those swords which the master sword maker gave to the villagers!

Chapter Three

The consequence of Europe's inventions

Some might be confounded by the fact that we do not consider Europe's inventions as the source of the world's ascendency and betterment and might thus not easily accept our views on this matter. For this reason, we begin again and cite other reasons:

This point must be well understood that Europe's inventions have had no other effect than changing the instruments of life. For example, the ancients needed to travel and traverse roads either to obtain life's necessities or as a result of campaigns or battles against each other. Until recent centuries this was achieved by four-legged animals or sailboats. Europe has invented in their place fast-moving automobiles, railroads, aero planes, and ships, and in order to accurately understand that this change of instruments has never benefited the world, we cite the following anecdote:

Ten years ago, a merchant from [the city of] Hamedan came to Tehran[2] with a horse-drawn carriage to purchase merchandise, spending eight days on the road. This year he travelled the same distance in two days. There is a difference of six days between this and the former trip but what benefit is in the difference for him! Can he spend those six days in Tehran in tranquillity and enjoyment? If he does that, will others among his Hamedāni colleagues who have also travelled to Tehran by automobile not surpass him after immediately purchasing their merchandise and returning? If our merchant also disregards his tranquillity and enjoyment and immediately makes his purchase and returns as well, does he make a larger profit from his trade on account of having travelled by automobile and made a speedy return? It goes without

---

[2] Hamedan is an ancient city in north western Iran. The capital city, Tehran, is 322 kilometres east of Hamedan.

saying that neither of these results will ensue, and there is no difference in these regards between the former and latter modes of travel for our merchant.

Let us leave anecdotes aside, I will pose some questions and you provide the answers:

That today voyages are taken by automobiles, railroads, and airplanes; messages are sent by telegraph and telephone and letters by post; farming and textile production is performed by machines and a hundred other such inventions are in operation, do people work one day and spend another [day] in relaxation and merriment unlike other epochs? No!

Do people today eat and sleep more than the ancients? No!

Has life expectancy increased in comparison to former times? No!

Have poverty and privation been uprooted and people live in comfort? No! On the contrary, the severity of these ailments has immensely intensified!

Have vengeance and enmity been removed from among humans so that they attempt to harass each other less [than previously]? No! On the contrary, its severity has increased daily!

Then what benefit has been gained from these inventions of which Europe boasts so much, bragging on in each corner of the earth with the boastful pretence of progress and superiority?

A tree must be judged by its fruit. Be these inventions what they are, what is their benefit to humans?

It might be claimed that riding automobiles, flying with aero planes, conversing over telephones from distances of hundreds of miles, listening to the radio and other such activities each by itself is a pleasure of which ancient peoples were deprived but of which we are beneficiaries and these inventions, even if they do not untangle the world's affairs, have furnished humanity with novel pleasures.

This claim is to some extent accurate and well founded. However, to judge fairly [it must be said that] those claims that deem European inventions to be the source of the world's goodness and the cause of its prosperity are all frivolous and absurd talk.

Further, all those inventions cannot be judged on the same premise. Some have not untangled the world's affairs; conversely, they have added a hundred new entanglements and have become the cause of millions of people's ruin.

Inventions that are meant for public use such as railroads, automobiles, telephone, telegraph, the electric light and the like bring gain and loss to the world in equal measure and unlike their reputation, as we have shown, have never added to people's peace and contentment. If some find pleasure in using these inventions, others feel sorrow for not having access to them.

But inventions that benefit the powerful alone, these are the source of the world's destruction, and the state of Europe today, which is the most fearful of states, cannot be but as the consequence of those inventions.

Let us assume that two persons are grappling and hitting each other on the head and face with their fists and a third person has arrived on the scene who carries a few swords. Now if this person hands each of the contenders a sword, the result will be nothing except that the battle will get fiercer and bloodier. And if he gives one of the two a sword and denies the other the same, in this case it is evident that this affair will be the fortune and triumph of one and the ruin and death of the other.

These novel European instruments are also either tools that work for everyone in which case their outcome is nothing but the severity of daily struggle and toil, or they are only accessible to the powerful and the owners of means of production in which case the outcome is the ruin of millions of families [with no access to these instruments].

Besides some praiseworthy medical discoveries, other European innovations are not worthy of boasting about or raising one's neck in glory [over them].

Chapter Four

The instruments have changed, the wars remain

Since mention has been made of swords and battles we can further illustrate our proposition by outlining the history of war.

We know that in the former centuries wars were fought with swords, arrows, spears and lances but today instruments have been invented compared to which the old instruments appear as children's play. This is where Europeans loudly announce that the technology of war has improved and astounding instruments have been invented.

If we judge this according to the science of mechanics, chemistry, and other technologies, then European masters have indeed created singular artistry. But if we look at it from the perspective of the benefit or harm to the world, the claim to progress is the most nonsensical of all claims. This is because the difference between modern wars in which novel machinery of homicide is employed with the wars of ancient times is nothing but the fact that today's wars promote the vending of bloodshed and murder and multiplied injuries and destruction. Specially, if in a certain conflict these instruments are in the hands of one group while the other side has no access except to ancient instruments, then the artistry of European masters will be [cause for] the most disastrous calamity for the latter group.

Our ordinary existence is also similar to a war, particularly in regard to the battles and struggles which have always existed among humans. The inventions of Europe as well – ranging from automobiles to railroads, airplanes, telegraph, telephone and the like – are mostly employed in the battle of life. These, too, are novel instruments in this everlasting daily battle.

Thus, these inventions are precisely akin to the appearance of cannons and guns and tanks and bombs which have no relation to the peace and happiness of earthlings. On the contrary, many of the inventions of Europe – as we have shown – are similar to that cannon and gun which are possessed by one group while the other side meets them in battle with nothing but arrows and swords and lances.

If these inventions were beneficial to the world's welfare, Europe could boast of the improvement and ascendancy of the world and hold its head high in pride. But now that we have the opposite outcome before us and witness how these inventions have only added to the toils of life while some of them have been the cause of the destruction of millions of families, is there still a reason to boast of the world's improvement?! While the world has thus been debased is it not reprehensible for some to claim superiority and to close their eyes to truth, to sneer at the ancients and their times which were inevitably better than our own?

If the point is scientific progress, we do not deny it but what relation does this have with the ascendancy and progress of the world? As we have said and Europeans themselves admit, the superiority and improvement of the world cannot be but with the peace and contentment of its inhabitants, otherwise let there be no scientific progress!

Since the world is devoid of peace and contentment in the presence of these advanced sciences and numerous European inventions, as we have said it is akin to a person who has put on glamorous garments and adorned himself with gold, sliver, and gems but at the same time is bereft of health, which is the sole aspiration in life, and suffers day and night.

With all the harm it has brought to the world and with its boastfulness, Europe is like the story of the imprudent wrestler who tore out the foundation of a house and caused the collapse of the roof on the residents' heads in order to showcase his strength and skill, bragging about his foolish action without feeling concerned about the groans of the buried residents.

Chapter Five

Europe uproots the world's tranquillity

It must be said again that the root of the world's problems is the struggle and conflict which is always looming among humans, each person finding his own benefit in the others' loss. This contention between peace and conflict in the world is oppositional so that each time one intensifies, the other lessens and every time that weakens, the other thickens.

The best thing that alleviates the severity of this struggle and aids in the welfare of the people is religion. What religion accomplishes in this regard nothing else can. Whatever the opponents of religion say, we have put irreligiosity to the test [and know that] it is the root of the world's troubles and the enemy of the welfare of its inhabitants.

We are well aware of what atrocities have been committed in the name of religion in the past. Nevertheless, we view religion as a necessity for the world and [we] eschew irreligiosity.

We have risen from Asia, the cradle of religions, and we know that when religion spreads in a community it acts, in the first instance, as a legislator, indoctrinating the believers with a series of beneficial and worthy commandments. In the second instance, it acts as a watchman that oversees the execution of those commandments to the letter whether in public or in private. In the third instance it acts as a mentor so that after a long time when people distinguish between right and wrong, they deem wrong action not only sinful but also the source of dishonour, and consider good deeds not only worthy of reward but also the cause of good repute. And it is from here that virtue, or its Persian equivalent chivalry,[3] which after religion is the strongest agent of goodness in the world, appears among the members of that

---

[3] Kasravi uses the Arabic derivative *sherāfat* for 'virtue' followed by its Persian equivalent, *rādmardi*. Both terms denote nobility, honour and righteousness.

community. In the fourth stance, it acts as a judge under whom the believers who consider good deeds as the source of God's appeasement and evil deeds as the cause of His wrath will be contemptuous of the committers of evil deeds and view them with disdain while they seek the company of the committers of good deeds and cherish them. And thus the righteous will find the reward for their good deed just as the wicked also meet the retribution for their evil deeds in this world.

All these effects of religion we have seen with our own eyes and we are happy that these relics have not completely disappeared yet and we can cite some reasons.

That in small towns and villages in Iran they revere a guest, whether known or unknown, more than their own life; that the opulent throw mass receptions several times a year in which destitute neighbours are invited [and fed]; that each person considers stealing from another's possessions the worst [type of] disgrace; that the poor and the desolate endure their poverty and desolation yet do not greed after the wealth of the affluent; that each person considers it his duty to aid the desolate and the disadvantaged; that traders and merchants do not feel the need for records or deeds in their dealings; that houses are often unlocked and yet few thefts take place; that despite the absence of orphanages no orphan goes without shelter – if all of these are not the outcomes of religion, then what are they the outcomes of?! What other educator or mentor have they had except religion?!

But in large cities where people have been contaminated with European mannerisms and ideas, such good deeds have been on a sharp decline and in their stead robbery, duplicity, falsehood, fraud, avarice and egotism have spread plentifully because irreligiosity from Europe has infected these cities.

From the day Europe set out to invent a few machines, it has risen against religion and has continuously axed at the trunk of that mighty cause of people's welfare so that now irreligiosity is one of the souvenirs that Easterners travelling to Europe bring for their fellow citizens.

Just like our inexperienced youth who, having passed a few exams and exited the primary school, arrogantly think that with their modicum of knowledge they have reached an elevated state and with all their incapacity and impotence they think themselves to be the able masters of all things and all people, [in the same way] the arrogant toolmakers [i.e. technologists] of Europe think that in their hands they have authority over the universe and that whatever they want done, will be done,[4] considering themselves in no need of religion – that source of the world's prosperity.

Europe is the master of machinery but utterly hopeless in distinguishing loss from gain in the world. During Europe's rise in the past two to three centuries, certain individuals have been recognized as liberal philosophers.[5] Read their works and see what poisonous and pointless claims they have effused by means of the pen! Claims that have no basis except in false thoughts but are useful pretexts for alienating people from religion!

As if they have been the enemy of humankind or have been envious of humanity's modicum of peace, determined to disrupt it; otherwise why would a philosopher not know that theoretical questions must be explained in such language that they do not lead to the misguidance of the gullible public? Why would he not know that the majority of the people do not have the restraint to cope with just any thought [spoken to them]?

Suppose that someone in his theoretical excavations found a certain truth or what he assumes to be the truth, must he not consider that the world's tranquillity is worthier than any pursuit and that he must not commit acts that breach the foundation of the world's welfare?

If a person candidly seeks the truth, he knows that in the boundless desert [of knowledge] in which he seeks, many a wise man has gone astray and has come to naught – he knows that in that desert there are salt pans that appear as water, and he will not be deceived by those distant phantasms and will not lead himself and others to destruction!

The world is more than ever in need of religion, and [achieving] the world's welfare is the most arduous of tasks except with the assistance of religion.

---

[4] This is a possible allusion to the Quranic phrase 'kun fa-yakun'. The phrase occurs several times in the Quran in reference to God's power to bring anything into existence by simply willing it to be, for instance, Quran 40:68 – 'He is the One who gives life and causes death. Then when He decides upon a thing, He says to it only: "Be," so it becomes'. Through the allusion, Kasravi intends to highlight the arrogance of 'the toolmakers of Europe' in considering themselves as Gods on earth with the power to will into being anything they desire.

[5] I have used 'liberal' as the equivalent to 'āzād andisheh' in the original. Literally meaning 'freethinking', the compound noun as Kasravi intends it refers to the secular-liberal spirit of European scientific modernity. Important to note, also, is Kasravi's use of 'philosophers'. The word is used here not to denote philosophy as it is commonly perceived (the study of the nature of knowledge, existence, reality), but in reference to natural philosophy, the domain of natural and physical sciences. By 'philosophers', therefore, Kasravi means natural philosophers, or scientists. His reference to Darwin as a 'philosopher' in the following pages occurs within this same context.

Humankind is like that lunatic who appears sober and wise for as long as he has the straightjacket of religion on. Once the restraint is torn away, he will resume his lunacy and no force can obstruct his mischief and harm. If the liberal philosophers of Europe had the slightest wisdom regarding the world's gain and loss, they would know that one must not meddle with this lunatic's shackles and not involve the world in his harm and mischief! They would know that humankind is better served being ignorant but unsullied rather than attaining knowledge but becoming predatory and devious.

Chapter Six

Can law replace religion?

Europe claims that irreligiosity can be amended with law and that is why in Europe legislation is among the important functions of the state.

We admit, too, that law is beneficial and necessary for the world. But it must not be concealed that not much can be achieved from laws alone. Europe's own experiment illustrates that despite the existence of many laws in that land, misdeeds are increasing daily.

The cause of this situation is evident: the majority of people evade the law as much as they can so agents need to be tasked with inspection. These same agents, if they harbour hopes of personal gain by breaking the law, will become accomplices to lawbreakers. It then becomes necessary to create laws for this situation and to appoint others as enforcers. Only the latter have a propensity similar to the former and the vicious cycle continues.

For instance, America enacts laws against thieves, which the police and the judge must safeguard. After a while it becomes apparent that many police officers and judges have been accomplices to the thieves. Of necessity, another law is created to regulate the police and the judges and certain other agents are appointed to enforce this new law.

But many of the latter also elude their duty and will join the partnership with the thieves.

This is why in America thieves have many factions and have elected chiefs for their faction and we read how people do not have peace and security because of them.[6]

---

[6] Kasravi is alluding here to the Prohibition era (*c.* 1924–38) in US history during which gangsters could operate with impunity and guarantee their profits by bribing law enforcement officials and politicians alike.

Unless people take an interest in each other's gain and loss, the implementation of law in their midst is a difficult task. And this interest cannot appear except with the aid of religion.

We read that American journalists have gone to the president and requested that strict laws be enacted against the thieves. The president has responded: we have tried this; we cannot prevent corruption with law; we must instil virtue in people![7]

This is very well spoken. But can we instil virtue in people without the existence of religion? Virtue is considering misdeed a disgrace and deeming virtuousness to be the cause of pride. Can this belief be expected of people with [the existence of] irreligiosity?

In short, where there is no virtue, enforcing the law is the most difficult task, and virtue does not appear except with the aid of religion. Thus, for law to take root and bear fruit, religion must be involved; otherwise from law alone the same result will ensue which has ensued from American laws.

Religion has another difference with law: the faithful avoid sin on their own accord while followers of law avoid crime out of fear: religion rules over all the organs of the faithful while law governs but the foot and the hand. Religion governs both in private and in public whereas law does not govern but in public. Religion is not only the warden that inhibits from reprehensible deeds but also a mentor that teaches good habits and also an advisor that encourages good deeds – but law has no capacity except that of a watchman.

If we consider that there is one benefit in law, there are ten in religion.

Religion is akin to organic health whereas law is like that medicine which is taken after illness. Those who uproot the foundation of religion and pin their faith on law are like the person who cuts off his functioning leg and fixes a

---

[7] Given the publication date of *Ethos*, here Kasravi is most likely referring to Franklin D. Roosevelt's campaign address on Prohibition in New Jersey on 27 August 1932. Part of Roosevelt's address closely resembles Kasravi's paraphrase: '[T]he methods adopted since the Word War with the purpose of achieving a greater temperance by the forcing of Prohibition have been accompanied in most parts of the country by complete tragic failure. I need not point out to you that general encouragement of lawlessness has resulted; that corruption, hypocrisy, crime and disorder have emerged, and that instead of restricting, we have extended the spread of intemperance. This failure has come for this very good reason: we have depended too largely upon the power of governmental action instead of recognizing that the authority of the home and that of the churches in these matters is the fundamental force on which we must build'. Franklin D. Roosevelt, Campaign Address on Prohibition in Sea Girt, New Jersey Online by Gerhard Peters and John T. Woolley, The American Presidency Project, https://www.presidency.ucsb.edu/node/289317.

wooden leg in its place. Or it is, as the ancients have said, like he who took the foundation of the wall to mend the roof.[8]

For collective welfare and happiness both religion and law are necessities. But religion is the foundation while law is the wall; if there is no religion, from law alone no result will ensue.

We should also say a few words about European laws:

As we mentioned, in each corner of Europe many laws are in operation, laws that have been crafted in the hands of scholars and experts and consulted on, clause by clause, by hundreds of representatives in the parliament. Even with these laws, we know the state of Europe's disorder today:

On the one hand, they throw [excess] grain in the sea, on the other hand, the pangs of hunger drive many people to suicide. In one corner millions of skilled youths are unemployed, in the other corner women are performing manly work next to men.

In one area the affluent are immersed in indulgence in their multi-story edifices while in the other thousands of homeless men and women spend their days and nights in the alleys and under stairwells.

This is to be entirely blamed on law. It must be said that as Europe has divested itself of the benefits of religion, it is also deprived of useful laws. What sort of a law is this, then, that has resulted in such disorder?!

What is more than anything the cause of fear is that these European laws have been created by the governments through parliaments in the name of people's welfare, and we see the outcome. Facing these governments and parliaments are bands of workers and the unemployed who are sorely disgruntled with Europe's current state, awaiting the opportunity to overturn the current situation and take control of the affairs and they have even drafted their own laws for that day, laws which are based on cynicism, vengeance and hostility to peace. Who knows what the state of Europe will be with those laws?![9]

---

[8] This is Kasravi's paraphrase from the famous saying by the thirteenth century Persian poet Sa'di in his *Golestān* 6:1: 'The sire wants the terrace embellished / While the house's foundation is demolished' (khājeh dar band-e naqsh-e eyvān ast / khāneh az pāyband virān ast). Abu Mohammad Mosleh al-Din ibn 'Abdollah Shirazi (pen named Sa'di or Sa'di of Shiraz) was among the greatest classical Persian poets. He enjoys canonical status and is known for his mastery of Persian poetry but also for his worldly wisdom in issues related to ethics and morality.

[9] Kasravi may be referring to competing ideologies such as socialism and anarchism that opposed liberal capitalism and that reached their peak in the decades leading to the Second World War.

Europe and the trials of its workers and unemployed is like the person who has fallen in water and is floundering for fear of life. Some persons on shore make an attempt to save him, but before this they have accumulated firewood and made a large fire so that as soon as they take him out of the water, they can throw him in the fire!

Until a few centuries ago the world was in a peaceful state, and if there were some defects, in the past few centuries they have disappeared. Thus, now that we are weary of this European movement and its results and want to change them, why not return to our former state?!

Europe with all its bragging about progress and supremacy in the world disdains a return to the state of a few centuries ago. But today the falsity of that arrogance has become apparent and of necessity it is in the world's interest to return to the state of former times. What is important is to avoid the deficiencies [of those times] as we will address this issue in its proper place below.

Chapter Seven

Europe's woes

Despite all the marvellous inventions of Europe – despite the great proliferation of sciences – despite the bragging about mastery and superiority in the world – the region itself is in a very wretched state.

Our aim is not [merely] to find faults with Europe. Instead we intend to shed light on the causes of its defects so that it can lead to the awakening of the East and perhaps Europe itself can benefit from our sympathetic reproof and attempt to remedy its affairs.

The state of the East in relation to Europe today is [akin to] the story of that caravan that has strayed from the main highway and has been trapped in a swamp in the desert, unable to free itself. A second caravan on the highway notices the former's silhouette in the distance and thinks that the real highway is the one the first caravan is treading. On this illusion, they mindlessly make haste to join the caravan gone astray, and though with each step they get farther from the highway and closer to their destruction, they cheer in ignorance and their hope [of finding the true highway] grows.

Thus, here a guide is needed both to awaken this group to their ignorant action, leading them back to the highway, and to help that group to free themselves from the quagmire.

As we have said, one of Europe's defects, perhaps its worst, is the spread of irreligiosity. There would not be any concern, if irreligiosity were [limited to] lack of knowledge of God and disbelief in the invisible afterworld because these are veiled secrets in every person's heart, and at any rate God does not need any person's acknowledgement or lack thereof. However, religion is the foundation of a series of valuable good deeds and worthy morals of which the irreligious are devoid.

We evidently see that wherever religion has been dethroned, honesty, righteousness, sincerity, hospitality, beneficence, and other good deeds have also lost their currency and in their stead thievery, dishonesty, deviousness, money-grubbing, and other ills have found currency.

And then as we have said all of Europe's hope is [pinned on] law, but law has no benefit without the existence of religion; Europe's own trials prove this claim.

Europe must either free its neck from the clutches of depraved priests or abandon the practice of Christianity, but not reject religiosity altogether. If there is a necessity for the welfare and contentment of the world, if the people must be sincere and virtuous, religion must be protected and attempts must be made for its spread. Unseating religion and hoping for the world's betterment is [akin to] expecting a blind eye to see.

Europe's other trouble is machines and factories. A few centuries ago when Europe had just embarked on invention and only a few machines had been invented, everyone thought that these instruments will lead to the welfare of workers, and every person nurtured hopes of a better future. But from the [ensuing] misery, after a short while everyone discovered the truth that these infernal apparatuses are the enemies of the world's peace. Every day the workers' wages decreased even as the numbers of the unemployed increased so that it has gotten to where things stand today which have brought woes across Europe.

Every great machine which exists in Europe and which is in operation is responsible for the blood of hundreds, perhaps thousands of families. It must be said that the machine is [akin to] a tree with a thousand and one fruits, a thousand of them bitter and poisonous and one of them sweet and delightful; unless a thousand innocent people eat those poisonous fruits and perish, this one sweet fruit will bear no benefit to the owner of the tree.

Europe has made these inventions the cause of its glory and prides itself in them to no end; not only does it look down on Asia and the East scornfully, but it also permits shameful [views] towards its own chivalrous ancestry. But we know full well that these inventions are the cause of the world's destruction, the reason being Europe's own woes today!

It is from these machines that the workers' wages have decreased so much that they cannot afford but peasant food for dinner and lunch. It is because of them that the unemployed in every corner of Europe are counted in the millions, each of whom with five or six household members is devoid of shelter and fodder and clothes and other means of subsistence and most of whom live on streets or under bridges.

This [itself] is a great disgrace to Europe, and we know that as a result of this condition of the workers and the unemployed, in every corner parties have been formed by them which are sworn enemies of the affluent and are always in search of an opportunity to uproot them. And that advocates of Europe in the East have given these parties a different meaning, admiring them as technologies of governance, is a lie which they have crafted in order to veil the deficiencies of Europe. We saw in our own time what the consequence of party formation was for Russian workers.[10] The same outcomes are also feared in other corners of Europe.

Another harm of the machines and the factories [is] that goods are made in excess of the people's needs, leading to inevitable stagnation in the markets. This is why the factories in every country aim to monopolize the world's markets and not allow other foreign industries to find [their] way there and rivalry and hostility ensues from this, leading to much bloodshed; such it is that the great war of over a decade ago and those infinite bloodsheds happened, and today again the fear of [another] war lurks for the same reason.[11]

Worst of all [is] that Europe has made commerce the centre and life the periphery. We all believe that commerce and trade are life's peripheries and in fact a way to provide the means of subsistence; in other words we seek commerce as a means to subsistence so that we can purchase what we need for livelihood but not purchase what we do not need. Europe has the opposite of this belief, considering trade and commerce the main end and life as a means to that end. More clearly, Europe demands people's livelihoods to [bolster] trade [creating a situation] in which people must purchase whatever goods it produces in its factories, whether they have a need for it or not.

This is why in European associations, whether official or unofficial, the discussion is always around ways to sell their commodity, not by [considering]

---

[10] Here Kasravi is alluding to the Bolshevik revolution of 1917 and the subsequent rise of the Soviet Union.
[11] The great war to which Kasravi refers is of course the First World War. The impending war referred to would materialize in the form of the Second World War.

which commodity is necessary or unnecessary for people's life and for their convenience, but even if people do not need certain goods, the clever industrialists of Europe devise a way to create that need. For example if instruments of war have been made but have not been sold due to the absence of wars, they will make a disturbance in some corner [of the world] and create a war so that they can achieve their goal. Or if there is a certain fabric or other useless goods, they provide the conditions for its consumption by encouraging and inviting [consumers to do so] or by creating laws [that would require consumption].

Many of the garments and toiletry or other things which we use today, [we use them] not because they have use in our life, but it is because the European factory which manufactures them finds ways to convince us to wear and apply them.

All this praise for cinema which they consider a means of good manners and a cause for the enlightenment of the masses and which they include in the fine arts, erecting academies for it, all of this is a lie and an exaggeration. On the contrary if we want the truth, this spectacle is futile and childish, weakens the eyesight and corrupts the morals, and those who continue to watch the spectacles, dysfunctions will appear in their brain.

The truth is that vast corporations have been established in Europe and America for film making through which they can make excessive profits, and they are the ones behind cinema's great popularity and spread.

If we heard that a certain cook in the bazar invites and encourages people to overeat because he has made excessive food and wants to sell all his meals without being concerned about people's health or illness, or if we knew that a certain doctor without reason incites people to buy and consume quinine because he has a large quantity [of it], we would inevitably unleash a hundred curses on that cook or that doctor and would not restrain our hatred or abhorrence. Then how is it that now that we see Europe's politics of trade which is exactly like that cook or doctor, perhaps more alarming and harmful, we never open our lips to criticize [them] but on the contrary bow in submission to those ignoble bands who have made a career out of advocating for Europe, elevating Europeans to the heights of honour?!

Note Europe's infatuation with commerce; it has reached such a level that one of the affluent persons there has said that factories must make insubstantial and flimsy products so that they quickly wear out and break, in this way amassing more capital so that the factories can continue to operate![12]

In the estimate of this affluent but depraved person, the goal of the world's creation is the continual operation of European factories and machinery and the masses have no other duty but to earn money through all manners of hardship so that they can frequently purchase goods from European factories!

Had the world [ever] witnessed such perversion?!

---

[12] In all likelihood, Kasravi is referring to a business pamphlet published by Bernard London, an American real estate broker, who in 1932 published a paper titled 'Ending the Depression through Planned Obsolescence'. London is credited with having coined the phrase 'planned obsolescence'. He proposed that any person who uses a product beyond its planned obsolescence (determined by the manufacturer) should be taxed. His idea of planned obsolescence was not legalized but continues to be practiced by some manufacturers. Kelly Brown, Planned Obsolescence in Technology: 1930s to Today, *The Information Umbrella*, February 2017, https://aimblog.uoregon.edu/2017/02/07/planned-obsolescence-in-technology-1930s-to-today/. (Last accessed January 2022).

Chapter Eight

What will be the consequence of machinism?

The truth is that Europe is caught in a bind from which there is no way out whether backward or forward, frantically taking such futile measures. This is because, on the one hand, everyone knows that the hefty load that Europe is shouldering will never reach its destination: the misery of millions of unemployed [persons], the factionalism and hostility between the destitute and the wealthy, increasing stagnation in the markets, daily surge in machinery and industries – these are problems that must be cured as soon as possible; otherwise Europe will face an utterly chaotic future.

On the other hand, it goes without saying that these problems arise from the machine and will not be resolved but with the abolition of the machine. But who will willingly do that and disregard the exorbitant and lucrative gains [from industrial enterprise]?! Or who will abstain from [using] soft and delicate fabrics or other exquisite machine made products and use handmade crafts instead?!

From the day humans have chosen communal life, each community has had its own measure for affluence, and generally there was not a considerable gap between the haves and the have-nots so that these two groups did not become completely cut off from or feel antagonistic towards each other.

But it is the result of machinism that in each European city the wealthy and the poor are so distanced from each other that they do not recognize one another and strive to uproot each other.

The factionalism and party politics in Europe follow similar suit as well. And that advocates of Europe give a different meaning to these groupings is a shameless lie because we know the affluent of Europe and how they take no account of the poor and never concern themselves with their misery, and even though the state of the destitute deteriorates day by day, they still claim ascendancy and superiority over the world, and even though it is possible to craft laws to remedy the poor's troubles, they never take a step in that direction.

On the other hand, we also know that the workers and the poor will not refrain from uprooting the wealthy if someday they find the opportunity, seeking revenge for the oppression they have endured.

The kind of division of labour which was widespread and still is in most cities in Asia has several benefits, benefits that cannot be achieved except through that same [old] order. In that division there is no trace of the plague of unemployment, and each receives his portion in accordance with his effort and ability. There are [still] the wealthy and the poor and the latter are [still] inevitably dissatisfied with their state, but there is no alienation and animosity between these two groups and they coexist as brothers, especially in regions where religion is prevalent and the people are observant of the permissible and the forbidden [as decreed by religion][13] in which case the gap between the wealthy and poor is inevitably small and the wealthy, in accordance with [the ordinances of] religion, have regard for the state of the poor and alleviate their suffering and hardships.

Besides, the act of work [versus wage labour] and engagement [in a pursuit] itself is the best instrument both for the people's enjoyment and happiness and for the refinement of their character, but machines not only sever the means to the workers' sustenance, they also deprive them of enjoyment, contentment, and good character.

If you ask a European person: 'What is the benefit of the machine for the world?' he will respond: 'For the convenience of the workers who did everything by hand before the invention of the machine'. If you ask again: 'What is the remedy for these millions of unemployed [persons]?' he will respond: 'Governments need to think of employment for them'.

This is one [example] of the paradoxical claims of Europe! Take your clue from this that Europe has abandoned wisdom and reason and immersed itself and others in such claims, oblivious to the fact that the universe is never bound by these paradoxes and what is destined to happen will happen.

---

[13] *Halal va harām* in the original text. These are Islamic concepts referring to righteous [halal] versus sinful [harām] action, applicable to a wide range of daily practices from earning a living to permissible food and admissible or inadmissible social relations.

If work is essential to workers, then the machine which has reduced the amount of work has been unfavourable not useful, it has been harmful not beneficial! If it is true that we must think of employment for the masses, then the machine must be eradicated instead of adding to its numbers every day!

The story of the machine and [its relation with] the world is [akin to] the story of that man who brought a tiger cub from the wild and resolved to raise it; he was so captivated by its stripes and brisk capering that the more it harried the neighbours and scratched their children's faces, the more pleased he felt and did not heed the warnings of the wise about the consequence of fostering such a brute.

After a while [the cub] started to inflict injury on his own children and wounded their faces.

His excellency then became exasperated and chained the cub and no matter how much the neighbours and his kin requested that he kill that fierce beast or return it to the wild, he did not heed [their advice]. Until one day he returned home from the bazar [noticing that] the neighbours had poured onto the street, each holding a spade or a stick tremulously and nervously staring at the walls and entrance to his house. Distraught, the esteemed man ran to the fore and enquired about the scene. When he found out [what had happened] he felt his insides clutch, gave off a bawl, and fell to the ground such that he never rose again. What had happened was that after his departure, the young tiger had torn the chains open and with a few leaps had drowned his wife and children in their own blood. Hearing their cries and groans, the neighbours had found out what had happened and thus poured out so that they may protect themselves and their children from that calamity.

It is the same with the machine: even though today it has ruined thousands of families and the number of its victims increases daily, no one is yet convinced that it must be abolished. After a while we won't see much beyond the passing of some laws to limit it to some extent. However, the final consequence of this hellish apparatus will be the same as that of the bloodthirsty beast.

Chapter Nine

What have the Prophets said and what does Europe say?

One of the reprehensible disservices of Europe is this call to 'Strive! Strive!' which it has echoed across the world. In Europe's estimation as soon as a person enters the realm of manhood, even from the time of childhood, [he] must have no other thought or aspiration except collecting money and amassing wealth, toiling day and night and on this path not shunning any scandal and not being concerned with anyone.

Mankind has enough greed and materialism in his nature. But since this nature is harmful to the world and to man himself, the prophets, who have been the healers of the world, as well as all the wise and the greats, who have worked for the good of the world, have all endeavoured to restrain the spread and severity of this [aspect of] human nature. However, in Europe's opinion this nature must be promoted so that every person endeavours without cease to obtain money and wealth without concern for anything.

We will cite an example so that Europe can understand its mistake and learn how it is axing the tree of the world's peace.

In a village there were two neighbours, one wise and the other ignorant. Each had several sons and a garden. One day the ignorant [person] calls his sons and tells them each to take a basket and pick some apples from the garden. One by one he emphasizes to all of them to try and pick more apples and to not return but with a full basket. Now if there were plenty of apple trees in the garden, there would be no concern and each son could choose a tree and pick apples in accordance with his effort and ability. But we know that in the garden there is but one apple tree. In this case the result of the father's emphasis will mean that when the sons arrive at the garden, each is determined to ward off the others so that he alone can climb the tree and pick all the apples. Accordingly, a fierce tussle ensues so that once any one of them approaches the tree, the others will assault him or if one crawls up, the others will seize his legs and drag him down. This struggle continues until twilight and everyone collapses groaning from exhaustion except one person who will pick the apples and return to the father alone.

The wise father also sends his sons to the garden to pick apples. But his recommendation to them is to treat each other in a brotherly manner and he whose strength is greater should not withhold his assistance to the others and anyone who picks more apples should share them with those who have picked fewer apples. These sons go to the garden and pass their day in joy and exuberance, returning home to their father at night feeling content and tranquil.

The imperatives that Europe issues to the world are akin to the recommendations of the ignorant father which achieves nothing but suffering and injury. Aye, if we sustained ourselves like the ancient times through cultivation and wool-spinning and similar activities, in other words if the basis of our sustenance was combating the world (nature), this European imperative to 'Strive! Strive!' would be beneficial, and the more effort people made, the more return they would get from nature's blessings. But now that the basis of our sustenance is battling each other, no other outcome but the toils of a gruelling life will ensue. Such that this has already happened in Europe and millions of people have succumbed [to it] and have no hope but death.

The people of the East have heard Europe's praises so much that they think it is heaven on earth and that its population lives in happiness and joy. Little do they know that in each corner millions of families have been driven to streets wandering and sleeping under bridges. Millions of people are unemployed and find the means of sustenance denied to them. Advocates of Europe themselves concede that sometimes the poor commit crimes to go to jail in order to receive [free] daily broth there.* It is said that the government in Budapest needed executioners. One hundred and fifty persons applied for this base profession, sixty of whom had graduated from institutions of higher learning.**

---

* A person who had travelled to Europe said at the Consultative Assembly that in Switzerland an old man had committed several crimes and had each time been sentenced to imprisonment for years. They asked him the reason and he responded, 'Since it is a difficult situation outside [the jail] but in jail they serve broth twice a week, to get that meal, the moment I'm released from prison I commit another crime to return to jail'.

** This is [according to] news released this year by one of the European [news] agencies.

What worse form of hardship is there?! This hardship has resulted from that imperative to strive, strive! Because where one must only work without being concerned about others, a group of the powerful will overtake [others] and monopolize all the means of sustenance for themselves while the others are left behind and end up in a situation where the greed for broth twice weekly drives them to commit crimes or stoop so low as to accept the basest of professions [that is, as an] executioner.

Those who [only] see the wealthy in Europe and America who have amassed millions in possessions in a short time and wonder at their exertion and acumen should also see that at the foot of their twenty and thirty-story edifices thousands of the hungry and the wretched have no choice but to submit to all forms of degradation and misdeed!

Those who praise America for being the land of enterprise and work should also ponder the eleven million unemployed there who, if we consider each as part of a family of four, [account for] fifty-five million of the residents of that country who have the means of subsistence denied to them!

The prophets advise that in the caravan of life there are those powerless people of whose [miserable] state you must be mindful. On this path which you tread, take mindful steps, travelling for a time and resting at others, so that neither you get exhausted nor the powerless are left behind. Conduct [yourselves] such that when your journey ends, you are not distanced from each other and can share the pleasures and comforts of the oasis together.

But Europe says that we must travel the path as fast as possible, even run, so that those who are powerless are separated and left behind, and if one of them has a stick to aid him in walking, we must pull it out of his hand and if another one has fallen, we must step on his chest and trample on him so that he cannot rise again.

We must conduct ourselves such that at the end of the journey no one is left standing in the caravan except the few strong and powerful persons so that the pleasures and comforts of the destination can be monopolized by these few.

This [is] the mandate of Europe and that [is] the command of the messengers of God.

You be the judge, which one is better and more beneficial to the state of the world?

Life in Europe today is exactly similar to the situation in which someone has escaped from the battlefield and the enemy is in pursuit such that this person can never rest nor sleep and [must] continuously run, and if he gets hungry, he eats his meal while on the run. A large number of people in Europe are also in this state such that they must work night and day or succumb to anxiety, not even resting during sleep. And if a person neglects [this condition], he will be left out of the cycle and lose the means of sustaining himself and his family and have no option but suicide.

Advocates of Europe constantly claim: 'In Europe time is precious!' Their intention is to praise Europe; however, it is not a matter of contention among the wise that the preciousness of time is itself the proof of the difficulty of life. The difficulty of life is in turn a defect for a community, not the reason for their nobility or superiority. Time is also precious in a battlefield because if someone is not cautious for a moment, the result could be the loss of his life. But is it possible to praise life on a battlefield and consider aggressors more superior?!

Chapter Ten

The Europist movement in Iran

We now leave Europe and return to the East.

For years a peculiar movement has appeared in the East, a movement that has no precedence in history. Easterners everywhere have risen and hurriedly try to make their own countries like Europe. They institute European laws and promote European habits and morality among their families. Men and women proudly fashion themselves in European style. The sole desire of every nation is to catch up with Europe before others do so that, as it is claimed, 'they can reach the caravan of civilization'. But they are all so disoriented that they trample on religion, piety, and morality, which are the most valuable treasures of the East.

We already said that such a shock is unprecedented in the history of the East.

This land [the East] has been the cradle of prophets and has taught religion to everyone the world over. How is it that it now considers religiosity and piety among the most inferior things?! How is it that it throws away in this manner valuable and commendable morals such as sincerity, chivalry, charity, hospitality, protecting strangers, beneficence, compassion towards the helpless, and contentment, each of which is the cause of goodness in the world and it will take hundreds of years of endeavour to spread such admirable principles [among people]? How is it that they used to be ashamed of mentioning women's names in a men's gathering but today they take their own wives and sisters to drunken dance parties? How is it that fifty-year-old men have learned to dance like women and consider it an art?!* How is it that a man who has

---

* A few have committed this frivolity in Tehran.

spent his youth in piety now at the age of eighty and on his way to the grave writes love stories?!*

Where has this movement appeared from and what has been its cause?

And what result will be gained from this endeavour and [this] wave? We will briefly explain the history of this state of affairs in Iran so that it becomes evident what hand has been involved and what results will ensue:

From the time that machines and industries multiplied in the West and the warehouses were filled with goods, Europe has viewed the East as a market for itself. In the previous century European states meddled much in every corner of the East and created disorder which, according to their own confession, has been only for advancing their trade policies.

They have also dispatched missions individually or in groups to Eastern cities with the same intent. However, their fortune has turned [for the better] ever since in the East itself movements have emerged in the name of acquiring freedom or Europism.[14]

As a case in point twenty-seven years ago the constitutionalist uprising broke out in Iran. The leaders of the uprising had become weary of the tyranny of the state and the powerful and of the disorder in the country. They demanded nothing more than justice and order, and they needed only a few exemplars from Europe. At any rate, the aim [of the constitutionalist movement] was never Europism.[15]

But from the very first day Europe's hand was involved and they manipulated a few of the leaders to espouse their cause; some others also joined their ranks out of ignorance.

---

* A man who has in excess of eighty years of age and used to be a prayer leader in his youth and still wears a turban translated [such] a story from Turkish and published it in one of the newspapers last year.

[14] Europism has been used as the equivalent to Kasravi's 'urupā'i-gari'. Literally meaning the state of being a European, Europism is a central concept in this book which Kasravi re-invokes numerous times in the rest of the text, but also in his later works which would appear after the publication of *Ethos*. It refers to a current of thought within the East that advocated for a full conversion of Eastern societies to European norms, from law and governance to modes of sociability, mannerisms and daily practices. In the following decades after Kasravi's demise, other Iranian intellectuals, notably Ahmad Fardid (1910–94) and Jalal Al-e Ahmad (1923–69), would reengage with this concept and reintroduce it as *gharbzadegi* ('Westoxication').

[15] Kasravi's reference here is to the Constitutional Revolution of 1906–7 in Persia, which led to the granting of a constitution by the then monarch Mozaffar al-Din Shah Qajar (1853–1907), turning Persia from an absolute to a constitutional monarchy.

This is why the fight for justice which was the basis of that movement, along with all the endeavours and sacrifices which were made in its name, suddenly turned into Europism.

After the uprising subsided and things were restored to normalcy, suddenly essayists and orators all over Iran claimed that the people were solely seeking Europism, and adoring Europe, they thus fabricated many lies and exaggerations.

According to these [writers and orators], Europe is the source of every virtue and excellence and Europeans, both men and women, are angels on Earth. Civilization, which is lacking all over the world, is an exclusive privilege of life in Europe and it must be delivered from there to other lands along with the automobile, the cinema, and the theatre. Iranians must acquire from Europe everything there, including law, morality, and custom. They must establish political parties in the manner of Europeans and be each other's sworn enemies. What else can I say about what these ignoble people have said.

Ultimately [their] conclusive view is that everything European is noble and elegant and everything Eastern is ignoble and vile. One of them has unveiled their intention and has insolently declared: 'Iranians must become European physically and spiritually, internally and externally!'[16]

At this juncture in every city the youth have graduated from schools, inexperienced and terribly misguided youth – youth [that are] like a drum: empty inside but loud. Out of ignorance and misguidance these [young people] take the advent of the history of the East as the day when the Europist movement has emerged and they count the preceding golden ages, times that dazzled the world, as nothing.

When unrestrained and emboldened, ill-bred and rowdy people will sacrifice the worthiest of people and the most precious of treasures for their own unbridled impulses. In the same manner, this handful of ignorant youths and that band of abject advocates of Europe, when they find the field open with no one to oppose them, they throw down and trample on the worthy heritage of the East, paving the way to Europism for themselves and others.

---

[16] Kasravi alludes to Seyed Hasan Taqizadeh (1878–1970) here. In an often-quoted proclamation, Taqizadeh famously declared, 'The only [solution is that] Iran must become Europeanized in appearance and in essence and in body and in spirit'. 'Dowreh-ye Jadid', *Kāveh* 5, no. 1 (22 January 1920), 1.

The only art these [people] have mastered is ridiculing and disparaging [Eastern modes of being], mocking everything, whether bad or good, and unleashing their reproof.

They have learned well that ridiculing and disparaging is the most poisonous weapon and that with this ploy the most rebellious person can be pacified.

When a wise person dons perfectly faultless and good garments, a few of them join voices each taking turn to ridicule that garment. That person with all his wisdom is repulsed by his own garment, takes it off and never wears it again.

[Even] the pelican which is one of the intelligent birds, if at the peak of its flight it hears children cupping their hands in front of their mouths and booing it, it loses heart, its wings will stop moving, and it will drop to the ground like a stone.

Poor simple-hearted Iranians suddenly found themselves amidst a ruckus, opening their eyes to see some people hard at work and joining their voices to criticize and ridicule every aspect of their existence from religion and morals to habits, speech, and behaviour. What they [Iranians] heard them say was: 'There is a land known as Europe which is heaven on earth and its people are like angels'.

If Iranians desire happiness and welfare, if they wish for improvement and superiority, they must become European inside and out. The more they listened to see whether someone says something different from these claims or criticizes one of these propositions, the less they saw [such] a person or heard [such] a voice and became bewildered. Taking one step forward and one backward [on account of being bewildered], they had no choice but to submit to the instigators' heart desire and follow them [the advocates of Europe] on the path to Europism. This is the brief history of Europism in Iran.

If the European governments had dispatched millions of troops to Asia and spent millions, they would not be able to move the East in this manner and pull them towards European lifestyle.

It is necessary here to cite a legend which comes from the Europeans' own books.[17] [The story is] in this manner: once the sun and the wind resolved to

---

[17] Kasravi is referring to the fable 'The North Wind and the Sun', attributed to the ancient Greek fabulist Aesop (*c.* 620–564 BCE).

battle each other, each thinking that its power is superior. At this point they noticed a lone rider in a desert and pledged to test their power on him so that whoever can take the rider's cloak off his back is more powerful. It was first the wind's turn to test its power. The sun hid its face behind the clouds and it suddenly got cold and a strong wind started to blow. The rider wrapped his arms around himself due to the cold and fastened the buttons on the cloak. And the stronger the wind blew, the harder the rider tried to hold the cloak and keep it in place on his body. The wind left the battlefield and it was [now] the sun's turn. It emerged from behind the clouds and it became warm again. Every moment [the sun] added to the heat and to [the severity of] its rays. The rider undid the buttons on his cloak and after gradually feeling the increasing heat, he took off his cloak and lay it on the horse's saddle. This is how the sun triumphed in the competition and it became known that warmth and gentleness can achieve what severity and harshness cannot.

The Europeans have done the same with the East. Even though they have no other aim but to find markets for their goods or in other words to plunder Eastern wealth, they do so under the pretext of science, civilization, progress and advancement, and with these pretexts and with the help of a group of base people, they uproot the foundation of the Eastern people's peace and induce them to abandon their modest mode of life.

Chapter Eleven

The East loses its treasures

In this movement of Europism the East perforce abandons certain aspects of its own life and takes certain things from Europe. Let us see what it loses and what it gains so that we can assess the benefits and the losses.

What is certain and we can witness with our own eyes [is that] religiosity, piety, charity, the consoling of the poor and the aiding of the deprived, modesty and other Eastern moral values have subsided and in their place irreligiosity, impiety, selfishness, pleasure-seeking, greed, short-sightedness, and combativeness prevail among the youth.

[There is] many a father whose source of pride was honesty but his sons today consider deceitfulness as their art. [There is] many a wealthy person who gave a share of his possessions to the helpless and the poor annually but his heirs spend money on nothing but self-indulgence. [There is] many an artisan, farmer, or worker who were content with the small sustenance they earned from their hard work and lived happily and never looked at the riches of the wealthy with the eye of greed or disloyalty, but today their children, as a result of the little learning they acquire at schools, have no other desire but wealth, and to achieve it they consider nothing a disgrace.

We have not forgotten the merchants of thirty years ago who wore simple outfits, lived simply, and the sole desire of any merchant was to gain reputation for piety and uprightness. And even though most trade was performed without a written contract, there was hardly any disagreement or dispute.

On the contrary, as soon as a merchant became somewhat prosperous, he opened his purse in endowments and donation, helped the poor, embarked on funding a bridge or a caravansary or a school, or he would print a book and distribute it among people, or he would finance someone's schooling, or he would dig a spring to provide water for a village and other such deeds for which we have much evidence in Iran.

We have not forgotten how keen merchants and other people of means in Iran were to throw feasts and feed the neighbours and the poor and how they took any good or bad event as an occasion for this deed. It was due to this open-handedness that the helpless and the poor could experience delicious foods. Even wandering beggars found their share and it never came to the point where, as in Switzerland, European people commit crimes to gain access to meat broth in prison.[18]

There were those who turned their homes into guesthouses and left its doors open to acquaintances and strangers alike.

There were wealthy [people] who would undertake to pay all the debts when they found out that a certain merchant or trader had become bankrupt, thus saving him from failure.

There were merchants who entrusted capital to others and commissioned them to trade, and there were many poor people who gained possessions in this way.

There were merchants who went bankrupt and their creditors would forgive the remainder of their claim. However, the merchant himself never accepted this indignity and worked and saved money for years and repaid the creditors' due.

But now there remains little trace of those good deeds. Today the wealthy and the merchants are those who have no desire but self-indulgence and self-adornment and spend money on nothing but what their own heart desires. In today's life only external adornment is creditable and everyone tries to amass money in any possible way in order to keep himself externally adorned with beautiful garments but no one is ever concerned with honesty or dishonesty.

Today spirits have become so debased that the wealthy neither leave behind charity establishments, nor do they care about the poor; they have no other intention except for their own pleasure and indulgence.

The best reason for the fact that the Europist movement is plucking the roots of uprightness and piety in Iran and that thievery and deceitfulness are increasing daily is that legal claims are on daily rise. And despite the existence

---

[18] While the precise source of Kasravi's claim here could not be located, many contemporary accounts exist of hopelessly unemployed people who would, out of desperation, commit petty crimes to receive minimal food and shelter in detention centres or camps during the Great Depression. John Steinbeck's acclaimed novel *The Grapes of Wrath* (1939), also set in the era of the Great Depression, contains similar accounts which paint a vivid picture of the relation between hunger and crime.

of sealed account books, disputes and disagreements among traders are several times more frequent compared to previous years.[19]

Europe greatly belittles the East.

Especially during the previous century when the raw fruits of inventions had not ripened and the veil had not been removed on the role of machines and factories, at that time every European thought of himself as being from a different essence and allowed [himself to apply] any kind of effrontery towards the people of the East. Read the books that Europeans wrote about the East in those times. See how they perceived the Eastern people and what faults they found. Leave the men aside, [even] a group of women who had come to the East as travellers and we do not truly know what profession they had and for what reason they wandered alone and without a guardian around foreign cities, even these have written books and found many faults with us. And unlike Easterners who praise everything European, Europeans belittle everything Eastern.

However, despite the Europeans' presumptions and despite the claims of a band of European advocates, the ancient and unglamorous East has invaluable inventories, inventories that are the foundation for the welfare of the world.

Even today despite all the steps which the East has taken towards Western lifestyle, our region has not completely lost its treasures, and still this region is in every respect superior to Europe and is more conducive to humanity's tranquillity.

The unseasoned youth and a bunch of advocates bewitched by Europe can view the worthy religion and piety and morals of the East in any way they desire – the wise know how valuable these treasures of the East are in the world's marketplace of benefit and loss.

These youths are the disgrace of their own time. These [youths] and their turning back from religion and piety is similar to a child or an ignorant person who receives a gem and, thinking that it is a [worthless] stone or [a piece of] glass, will trample on it.

But the wretched who have rendered their hearts to Europe, who include Europe in any discussion and embark on praise and exaggeration and in

---

[19] Kasravi makes this claim based on personal experience. During the 1920s and 1930s, he had served intermittently as judge and inspector-general in various provinces within Iran while later, after resigning from the Ministry of Justice, he started a private practice as a lawyer.

every conversation place the Iranian and the European on the evaluative scale, treacherously giving more weight to the European plate, these are either mercenaries of European companies or hate their own land and home; otherwise [the notion of] European superiority and distinctiveness is the cheapest babble.

These people disturb the simple and peaceful life of the Eastern people with their lies and exaggerations, ruining their tranquillity; their story is similar to the owl which in the darkness and quiet of the night, when the people have retired peacefully in their houses, as if being envious of the peace and contentment of the humans, it causes shivers and disturbance in [the people's] hearts with its sudden and untimely cries.

Chapter Twelve

What is civilization?

In provoking the people of the East into Europism, the advocates of Europe resort to certain pretexts one of which is civilization. According to them civilization is exclusive to Europe and from there it must reach other lands together with automobiles, theatres, cinemas and other such things.

We will write about the meaning of civilization and the way in which it emerged so that it is known that this handful of European advocates has either abandoned wisdom and intelligence and madly blurt out some claims or [they are] an ignoble group who destroy the foundations of the tranquillity of the East with their espousal of Europeans.

In very ancient times humans were scattered in forests and mountains and each clan chose a corner and lived far from the others. And because there were no rules or regulations, whoever could get the better of another would kill him and take his wife and children and belongings as booty.

This is why in fear of each other [ancient humans] could not settle in one place and were constantly fleeing or migrating. And because this manner of living was difficult and intolerable, some wise men rose and each gathered some clans around himself and made pacts to co-exist as brothers, withdraw the hand of thievery from each other's life and belongings, and not withhold their support and assistance from each other.

This development had positive results and humans were relieved from the hardships they had experienced. Gradually this type of coexistence spread everywhere and since this manner of living deserved a different name to distinguish it from desert dwelling, they called it 'city-dwelling'.[20]

---

[20] Kasravi's coinage is *shahri-gari*. This infinitival compound is composed of 'shahr' (city) and the suffix '-gari' which denotes 'to be' or a state of being. In this sense, Kasravi's coinage can be translated as 'the state of being in a city' or 'civility'. Thus, depending on the context in which the term is used in the original Persian, it has been translated in the following pages as either 'city-dwelling' or 'civility' alternatively.

The reason for this remark is that the term *civilisation* which is the name given to this manner of living in European languages derives from the word *civil* which in Latin means city. Also, the term *tamaddon* which is used in this sense in Persian comes from the word *madineh* which in Arabic carries the sense of city.[21]

This is the meaning of civilization and the manner of its emergence. It is evident therefore that civilization is not a new phenomenon and has been linked with human life from time immemorial; [it] is not exclusive to Europe, rather it is inclusive of every place. According to the Europeans' own admission, this type of living first started in Asia and from there spread to other lands, as the history of ancient Asian civilizations is famously testified to in European Orientalists' own books [on the subject].

Asia is the cradle of religion. Prophets have risen from here and brought numerous commandments, each of which was the source of the world's tranquillity for hundreds of years. Is the land from which Zoroaster, Jesus, and Mohammad rose devoid of civilization?! Sealed be the mouth that opens with such a claim!

Compare the laws of Europe with the simple guidelines of the prophets [when placed] on the evaluative scale of the world's benefit and harm. Which plate is weightier? The result of the prophets' dictums has been those worthy and valuable morals which we have already enumerated. The outcome of European laws is likewise the state of Europeans today: one group immersed in indulgence, while throngs of others [are] in the worst of states; a law whose yield is this does not deserve to be called law!

With all its self-promotion, Europe is not at the same level as Asia in recognizing the world's benefit and harm and in striving towards the well-being of its inhabitants, even though the Europeans and a bunch of their advocates have loudly filled the world with the boast of Europe's transcendence and superiority.

If by civilization, which is said to be exclusive to Europe, it is meant machinism and novel inventions, this is a greatly frivolous statement. This

---

[21] The italicized words in this paragraph appear as such in the original text. The French word *civilisation* is used for civilization; the Persianized Arabic loan-word *tamaddon* for civilization; and the Arabic word *madineh* for city.

is because inventions are the basic instruments of life while civilization has existed for hundreds perhaps thousands of years before their appearance.

On the other hand, if we don't [mean to] evade the truth, Europe, as a result of its inventions in the past few centuries, has lost the essence of civilization. Since it is in that land of inventions which great masses of people are bereft of any peace and even though the difficulty of their labour increases daily, the wealthy and powerful who pull all the strings never pay attention to them and are in pursuit of their own capitalist interests.

Civilization or city-dwelling does not [simply] mean living in cities, just as Bedouinism does not [only] mean dwelling in the desert.[22] In any place where a group of humans can extend their hand in oppression of others, depriving them of peace and happiness, that place is a desert and its inhabitants [are uncivilized] Bedouins – whether this oppression and taking away of others' peace be accomplished through war or with the aid of swords or silently through the invention of machines and establishment of factories!

If a highway robber invents a machine with which to strip travellers of their belongings, is he not a highway robber?! Or if a thief committed his robbery with the aid of scientific equipment, is he not a thief?!

The socialist movement which has mass following in Europe considers capitalists and the powerful as thieves and their possessions as stolen property. Can one find civilization in such a thieves' marketplace?! The goal of civilization is for humans to co-exist in a brotherly manner and not withhold their support and help from each other.

In a place in which people must engage in factionalism where this [political] party considers the others as thieves and feels animosity towards them while the others [in turn] step on this party and mercilessly trample on them, in this place what can never be found is civilization.

In a place where as a result of disorder, on the one hand, [excess] grain is thrown into the sea while, on the other hand, people commit suicide out of

---

[22] 'Bedouinism' is the coined equivalent to Kasravi's own coinage *biyābāni-gari*. Similar to Kasravi's other coinage *shahri-gari* (see first note in this chapter), the compound *biyābāni-gari* denotes the state of being in the desert, away from the city's civility. In this context, the term connotes the state of living in the desert, characterized by chaotic existence, absence of civil laws, resorting to raids for sustenance and revenge for justice, all of which, as Kasravi envisions it, connotes the state of being uncivilized.

hunger[23]; in a place where the wealthy take trade and capitalism as the principle and people's sustenance as a peripheral issue; in a place where millions of strong [but] unemployed youths are idle while women take on manly jobs – in a land where life is based upon sustained efforts for the accumulation of money without regard for others, civilization is many miles away!

If anything could be achieved through exaggeration and lies, [then] Europe could be the epicentre of world civilization, but which exaggeration or lie is not proven insufficient and does not pale before the truth?!

The state of Europe is akin to the person who does not admit that he is aging because at some point he was young and strong, still considering himself young and strong, even at the end of his old age and the hardships of incapacity – he still speaks of youth and strength.

Over a century ago, subsequent to a string of riots and revolutions, Europe crafted just laws and experienced a happy age. At that time Europe considered all people free and equal and fraternal and it was justified that [Europe] would pride itself in its civilization and speak of ascendancy and supremacy.[24] But now there is little trace of that happiness and nobility; the state of Europe today is more fittingly the cause of every European's shame.

---

[23] Throwing out or destroying crops and livestock was common practice in Europe and the United States during the Great Depression. It was thought that this strategy will stimulate the economy by keeping supply low and leading to increase in prices. In the United States, for instance, as part of Roosevelt's 'New Deal', the Agricultural Adjustment Act authorized the government to carry out 'emergency livestock reductions'. Farmers were paid to destroy their crops or kill their livestock while hundreds of thousands of unemployed people went hungry daily (also chronicled in Steinbeck's *The Grapes of Wrath*). Critics today point to alarming parallels between the Great Depression and what the International Monetary Fund has called the 'Great Lockdown' in our own time. For examples of the global practice of destroying food products during the Covid pandemic, see Suyin Haynes, "'The Saddest, Bitterest Thing of All." From the Great Depression to Today, A Long History of Food Destruction in the Face of Hunger', *Time*, 28 May 2020, https://time.com/5843136/covid-19-food-destruction/

[24] Kasravi is alluding to the French Revolution of 1789–1799 with its ideals of liberty, equality and fraternity.

Chapter Thirteen

European sciences

Another pretext for the advocates of Europe is the progress in sciences. In this respect, too, they have surpassed absurdity and no day goes by without their informing the people of the East of a novel invention or discovery or [without] parading the achievements of this doctor or that professor before the people.

We know as well that in the recent few centuries the sciences have had considerable progress in every field in Europe, but can one consider any science useful and acceptable? Can one be proud of the advancement of sciences that have produced bombs, tanks, and homicidal gases?

From time immemorial science has been a traveller such that in different epochs it pitches its tent with a certain group [of people] and gathers supplies [for its next excursion]. One day it erected its tent in Egypt, another time in Greece and the next day with Iranians and Arabs. Today it has set up tent in Europe.

Part of the sciences that Europe has monopolized today is the result of the toils of the ancients; Europe has also added a remarkable part to it. At any rate the sciences were beneficial and appeared harmless as long as they had not fallen into the hands of Europeans; but contemporary science is more harmful than beneficial.

It is true that in Europe sciences such as medicine, astronomy, history and the like have made considerable progress, but sciences from which those infernal apparatuses spring forth have developed and spread severalfold.

On the contrary it must be said that the benefits of the European sciences, with the exception of medicine, are more a matter of publicity than truth.

Once someone discovers some factual evidence, he adds to it from his own imagination. This is why in these sciences there are many claims analogous to the Jewish myth of the calf and the sea creature or the hypothetical heavens of Ptolemy the Greek.*

Leaving other sciences aside, in regard to the history and language of Iran with which we are well acquainted, we can clearly see that in these two fields the claims of European scientists have no basis but in fancy, especially in the science of language in which European scientists are utterly wanting and superficial, and even though they are at the same level as an abecedarian child, they claim mastery [in this field]. From this we can grasp the state of the other sciences.

And furthermore the rest of these sciences are the fruits of the toils of those scientists who lived prior to this [European claim to scientific mastery] and who had no other intent from their endeavours than knowledge and discovery.

In other words, they had an interest in science for its own sake and sought the truth. In today's Europe such people are a rarity.

Today there are few who have any purpose other than amassing riches. And if some people pursue the sciences, they only have an interest in them as a means to wealth. This is why the number of infernal apparatuses is on the rise daily, instruments from each of which the inventor and the few wealthy [investors] find immeasurable profits while the world gains nothing but harm and destruction.

Let us conclude: as we have said what the world needs and wants is the welfare of its inhabitants, and if we imagine this welfare to be a house, religion would be its foundation and the sciences the adornment on its walls.

Thus, Europe is the person who has damaged the house's foundation while priding himself on the adornments on the walls!

---

* As an example, [note the similarity to these myths of the theories of] the fire within the earth or the canals on planet Mars. [Translator's note: Kasravi's reference to the Alexandrian astronomer and mathematician, Ptolemy, in this sentence is meant to highlight mythical paradigms of thinking within what is considered 'science' at the time. Ptolemy's example is invoked to point to the fact that the Ptolemaic geocentric model of the heavenly bodies (established circa 150 CE) was the accepted paradigm in the science of astronomy until the Copernican revolution in the sixteenth century. Invoking 'the Jewish myth of the calf and the sea creature' (Behemoth and Leviathan featured in the Book of Job) serves a similar function. Scholar of the Hebrew Bible and one of the early proponents of an evidence-based approach to biblical studies, Umberto Cassuto (1883–1951), for instance, pointed out that a certain amount of mythology must be allowed in 'scientific' investigations of the Old Testament. According to Cassuto, the Torah 'should be studied against the background of the myths current in the Orient, as well as ... the ancient epic poems of the Israelites. The peoples of the East used to tell many stories about the battle waged by one of the great gods against the deity of the sea'. It appears that Kasravi is referring to this myth here. Umberto Cassuto, *A Commentary on the Book of Genesis: Part One* (Magnes Press, Hebrew University, 1961–64), 36.]

The adornment of humanity is religion and piety. He who is bereft of this adornment but is, as it has been said, an impious scholar is akin to a thief who commits robbery with [the aid of] a lantern, [an act] whose harm will inevitably be several fold.

If the sciences, in the manner they are practiced in Europe, were beneficial, that region should have become heaven on earth. [But] the state of Europe today is the best testimony that from those sciences bears forth nothing but harm and of them grows for humans nothing but disgrace.

It is neither becoming of science nor advantageous to the world that the sciences have become widespread and scientists increased in number while some of them are devious and make use of knowledge as an instrument for thievery and deceit while scores of people remain unemployed and hungry and stoop to the lowest of occupations.

Scores of Westerners are spread throughout Eastern cities and we witness that they have no aim but amassing money while exploiting the love and kindness of Eastern people, which they show any foreigner, to their advantage, [using it] to better achieve their objectives.

Many of them have added scientific titles to their names such as Doctor or Professor, and yet they have an ignoble nature, embracing the basest of crimes which include thievery and deceit.

This by itself is a disgrace to Europe that it has incited people to degeneracy and impudence instead of leading them to beneficence and sincerity with the aid of science. Of Europe's deviance it suffices to mention that it deduces irreligiosity from science. What all those polytechnics, those academies and institutions of learning have promoted abundantly is irreligiosity, impudence, and manipulation.

It is a wonder that the makers of machinery in Europe have risen in a crusade against the prophets. Prophets who, according to Europe itself, rose at the darkest hours and enlightened the world with their religion. Prophets whose teachings are still more beneficial to the world than the laws of Europe.

That we mention the makers of machinery is because Europe's chief feat is making machines and it is on this basis that Europeans, who have risen in enmity to God and religion, have gained fame as philosophers; otherwise most of what they have said is the most meaningless talk.

If we require a parable for [demonstrating] this proposition, [this] can be said: Someone is severely ill and a physician has embarked on his treatment, prescribing regimes which he [the patient] must regularly follow. Meanwhile a blacksmith makes iron tools such as a spade and a pickaxe and an axe and sends it to the patient and expects him to consider him [the blacksmith] superior to the physician and to follow no prescriptions but the orders of the master blacksmith [simply] because he has shown great craft in making those tools.

On the question of the world's gain and loss, Europe with all its crafts and knowledge and despite all its inventions and discoveries is nothing but a master ironworker inasmuch as no other result has been gained [from its inventions] but a change in the tools of daily life. But the prophets have been the physicians of the world insofar as they have said the world's ailment is that disastrous battle which is always afoot among humans and the prophets have attempted to cure this ailment and have established tenets which alleviate the severity of that ailment and bring about the welfare of the world. And that Europe, conceited with its inventions, does not approve these tenets and criticizes them is precisely [akin to] the story of that physician and that blacksmith.

Chapter Fourteen

Women should not be wayward

A few words should be said about women[25] as well since women are also one of the pretexts which is always mentioned [in the Europists' arguments], and everywhere scores of women have been stirred and are in their own estimation striving for the betterment of women's state.

Here, too, the weapon is mockery and reproach through which advocates of Europism disparage and ridicule all things related to the Eastern woman and praise all things related to Western women so that many youths shun marriage to Eastern women and bring wives from Europe, considering this linkage with Europe an honour.

We know that in the East women are considered inferior and treated with injustice and there is no denying that women should be treated better than Easterners treat them. But we should never follow Europe [in this regard]. On the contrary it must be said that the habits of Europeans in regard to women are flawed and reprehensible like many other of their practices. If our treatment of women is bad, the Europeans' treatment [of them] is worse.

---

[25] The content of this chapter does not reflect the full spectrum of Kasravi's evolving views on women and their social role, particularly for readers who may not be familiar with his other works. A more detailed exposition of Kasravi's views regarding women can be found in his *Khāharān va Dokhtarān-e Mā* (Our Sisters and Daughters), first published in 1944. In this book, Kasravi makes it amply clear that he opposes the hijab (head covering) for women, considering it as a limit to women's full participation in society and arguing that viewing the practice of hijab as an Islamic ordinance is in fact a falsification of the true teachings of Islam. He also condemned polygamy as a social ill and denounced cultural norms that attached a moral stigma to a woman's sexual affairs but did not hold a man's similar affairs to the same standards. He advocated for women's right to divorce and championed other rights for women such as the right to education and work, not to mention his endorsement of women's suffrage and active participation in the politics of their country as informed citizens. He scornfully considered as backward cultural practices that were based on a false belief in women's lower intelligence in comparison to men and regarded women as having equal, if not higher, intelligence to men. Kasravi did, however, believe in prescribed gender roles that would limit women to only certain types of 'womanly' work or education and held that women should be subservient to their male guardians and should not mingle with strange men without their guardian's consent. While he rejected the European notion of 'women's rights', he advocated for women's liberation within certain prescribed frameworks.

First, we must consider if women are the same as men in every respect. From what we know a woman, no matter how intelligent and wise, is weak compared to a man and incapable of protecting herself. From this [it follows that] every woman needs to have a man for her guardianship and protection and a woman should never be wayward.

A woman should not be wayward not because she is inferior and worthless but because most men are scoundrels and sinful.

Waywardness for a woman is [akin to] a desert where she will face none but seductive ghouls – it is [akin to] a balky horse which of a hundred women not a single one can tame and shall fall flat to the ground! A wayward woman will not only herself be undone and disgraced, her harm will also extend to other families. Those who let their wives loose should not hope for a respectable future for themselves.

Beauty and charm are a woman's assets and if she safeguards them and does not give those assets away for free, she will always live happily. Otherwise those same assets will be the cause of her undoing.

A woman can steal a heart but she cannot retain it. A man sees a woman, is captivated by her, and inexhaustibly pursues her. This is a story that happens every day and everywhere several times. On such occasions if a woman has a [male] guardian, the story ends in a marriage contract and family life begins. But a wayward woman will not take anything from this story except disgrace and many a woman has ruined her future in this way.

In other words, a woman should bestow her God-given assets which are her beauty and youth upon he who will undertake the duty to protect and safeguard her. However, a wayward woman can rarely avoid the deception of highway robbers and thieves and squandering her God-given assets.

In any case for as long as a woman is a maiden, her care should be in the hands of her father or her older brother and when she enters wedlock with her husband she must seek the husband's approval and take his permission as guidance for whom she socializes or associates with.

A married woman must be aware that there is many a highway robber on her path and she cannot be protected from their harm except with the aid and support of her husband. The husband must also respect his wife and safeguard her and prevent her from associating with anyone who is not trustworthy or righteous, and [he] should always accompany her.

Beware that no woman mingles with male strangers in the absence of her father or husband! Any father or husband who permits his daughter or wife to associate with males or who takes her to any [such] gathering will be the cause of any blunder she commits and the blame falls on this man more than on that woman.

If we want the family to be the foundation of our life, if we want resentment and estrangement not to take the place of affection and harmony, we must take caution not to be deceived by European manners and guard our daughters and wives.

It is out of ignorance that they say if women and maidens are free to socialize and mingle with men, any man or woman whose intention is marriage can assess the other and make an informed decision to enter the matrimonial contract. This is because in those [types of] gatherings who has the opportunity for assessment and trial?

In those types of rowdy gatherings whence the presence of the wisdom to distinguish between right and wrong? Or for which man or woman is it difficult to temporarily conceal their shortcomings and not present themselves as they really are?! Or can a naïve maiden distinguish between the good or bad [intentions] of men and select a husband on the basis of [accurate] assessment?!

If women's freedom and their mingling with men had a beneficial effect, why are families in Europe itself engulfed in decadence? Why is there resentment between wife and husband and the phenomenon of divorce more common there than in Eastern cities?!

In Europe a great many men do not have wives and seek gratification in impure ways and in each city thousands of women and maidens have been left displaced and without a custodian and seek a husband. The scandal is so widespread that a separate book needs to be [written] in admiration.[26] And yet the Europeans praise their own manners while opening their mouths in reproach of the East! [This is] exactly similar to the [allegorical] crop-eared person who always applauded the joy of being crop-eared and wished for all to be crop-eared like him!

It is true that disregarding a woman's wish or accepting a man as husband without knowing him are not judicious acts and a woman should not be given

---

[26] It appears that Kasravi is sarcastically using 'admiration' for 'admonition' in this sentence.

to a man [in marriage] before she has an opportunity to know him. But for this knowledge and selection, a few visits between the relatives are sufficient and we must never allow European-style mingling for [our] girls and boys. At any rate in a girl's marriage contract there must be the father's or older brother's endorsement. Sometimes there is also talk of women's work and profession so that our women undertake manly work like the European [women]. But this expectation is very foolish. A woman should do work but not manly work. Just as women were created separately of men, their work is also separate. Homemaking, raising children, sewing, cooking and the like are appropriate types of work for women. As well a woman can be involved in her husband's or father's profession and assist him [in it].

That in Europe women work side by side men is for one of these reasons: some are not observant of chastity and wish to find pleasure by mingling with men and brushing shoulders with them, or [they] wish to combine business with indulgence.

Others have been placed [on display] in stores by their fathers or husbands in order to attract more shoppers and promote sales. A third group is composed of women who have no guardian or family and out of desperation have had to do the men's work to earn a living. The fourth group are women whose husbands cannot find work at the factories so they have undertaken labour instead of their husbands. Or if the husbands also work, since the workers' wages are too meagre and cannot sustain household expenses, the women also have to work.

The working of women is one of Europe's deficiencies, a shameful deficiency! Is it out of respect for women that they separate her from her child and house and force [her] into unbearable manly work?! Is it not the sign of a people's ignorance that they rip children out of their mothers' arms, stuff them in formations like dumb cattle and send them to kindergartens; eat their lunch and dinner at the market instead of [having] healthy homemade meals; and leave their houses to the care of maids instead of housewives[?] They do all of this so that they can employ women for business activity at the stores!

Those who wish these shameful perversities upon the East and the Eastern woman, unless their pretext is witlessness and ignorance, they must be called enemies of the world's welfare!

About women's education as well today they adhere everywhere to [the model of] Europe. But this will have no outcome except remorse. Women should be educated in fields that help them in homemaking and raising children, such as medicine, midwifery, hygiene, sewing, cooking, weaving, and the like.

What must be said at the end is that a woman's adornment is her chastity. Unchaste women must be despised and abhorred except those without a guardian or [those who] slipped and became unchaste due to their husbands' or fathers' ignorance. Those wretched [women] must be forgiven and it is everyone's duty to extend a supportive hand to fallen women and help them out of the pit of impurity.

But more impure than these unchaste women are those men who do not take a wife and do not shoulder the responsibility of running a family and are constantly seeking to seduce women and girls. This perversity is yet another souvenir from Europe and it is often from such impure people that cries of women's freedom are heard.

It must be emphasized again that no matter how impure women of ill repute are, these [men] are more so. No matter how despised the former are, these [men] must be despised more.

Not having a wife is itself a sin and those who do not take a wife must be considered as sinners and disgraceful and [must be] despised and [they] must not be allowed entry into houses and gatherings, especially to those gatherings and houses where there are women. If a law should make marriage mandatory, in this way a large part of [the problem of] depravity in our time will be solved.

Chapter Fifteen

A leader does not lie to his own people

There is a saying among Arabs: 'A leader does not lie to his own people'.[27] Among the Arab Bedouins who migrated from place to place each tribe chose a person from among themselves to move ahead of the tribe and to look for an oasis with water or a pasture secure from thieves and highway robbers and then to return and lead the tribe to that place. This was a very important task and the leader never lied to his tribe because his lie would harm the tribe and he himself would receive a share of the harm.

Those who move ahead of the East's caravan today, guiding it towards the Western lifestyle, would that they had as much honesty as the desert dwelling Arab guides and not lie to their own kin, showing Europe as it really is and giving people the freedom to choose whether to follow Europe or not.

Would that next to having so much hyperbolic praise of the West they enumerated a few of its defects as well. Would that they said that Europeans are those who want the world and the people in it only for the expansion of their trade, and wherever their trade policies dictate they would not hesitate to shed the blood of millions of people and to uproot thousands of families. Would that they said that a majority of Europe's learned have, from all their knowledge, surmised that thievery and manipulation does not equate dishonour. Would that they asserted that the philosophers in the West

---

[27] It is not clear what the precise source of this saying is. However, almost certainly Kasravi has in mind the ethical and moral code of conduct known as *futuwwa* (youth, manliness) among Arabs. A corpus of fraternal rules and ideals (similar to the European notion of chivalry), *futuwwa* served as an organizing and cohering system of communal coexistence, especially in the absence of a strong central authority, such as in pre-Islamic Arabia or, in later centuries, in the power vacuum created during the fall of a dynasty. Some of the ideals within the *futuwwa* included generosity, hospitality, charity, sacrifice, heroism, perseverance and courage. There was considerable cross-fertilization between the Persian concept of *javānmardi* (which Kasravi references later in Book 2) and the Islamic notion of *futuwwa*, which like its Persian twin also carries the literal sense of youth and manliness.

have come to believe that millions of the unemployed and the dispossessed must be annihilated and [that] their situation must not be remedied until they perish.[28]

Would that they said that in Europe no sign is left of the ethos of humanity. This is because in every [Western] nation millions of individuals are in the direst of situations while others who are jocund and prosperous pretend that they do not see their dire situation, filling the world with boasts of improvement and superiority. Would that they disclosed that in America thieves have organized bands which the state is helpless to contain, that in that civilized land some people commit crimes [solely] to enter prisons and receive [the jail's] broth.

Would that they revealed that in every [Western] city hundreds of engineers and doctors and professors are unemployed and [that] only in Budapest sixty of such cultivated individuals have volunteered to become executioners [simply to have a job].

As much as they have contributed to the popularity of the socialists, would that they also said that if one day the state's affairs fall into the hands of these [socialist] parties, that day Europe will be entirely in flames and a picture of inferno. That day humanity's madness and savagery will reveal itself in its entirety.

As much as they parade European patriotism before [our] people, would that they also revealed that this patriotism is nothing more than the fact that whenever there is a war, the French are thirsty for British blood while the British slaughter the Germans audaciously and the Germans exterminate the Belgians recklessly. This rancour and enmity is the result of those bloody wars which nations waged against each other in centuries past and have been recorded in their histories. Otherwise, in Europe there is never patriotism in the true sense of the word because in every [European] nation millions of men, women, and children are weary of poverty and desolation while hundreds of others commit suicide out of hunger, and yet their compatriots do not empathize with them and do not contemplate a remedy [for this situation] even though they can amend all that misery with some laws.

---

[28] This is an early reference to social Darwinism, to which Kasravi returns several times in the following pages.

That man who wants Iranians to be Europeanized bodily and spiritually and internally and externally, would that he disclosed what Europism is and would reveal [the essence of] his wish.

What is Europism? Amassing money, dandyism, self-gratification, and nothing else!

The prophets' teachings dictated that whoever [was] more righteous and did greater good deeds was considered more respectable and worthier. In ancient Eastern way of life, too, according to this ethos those who desired respect and honour sought to be more pious and do more good deeds. Or when they were pious and performed good deeds, [even] if it weren't to please God, it was to protect their own honour and respect [for which] they stringently avoided harassing others and did not taint themselves with knavery and deceitfulness. [Instead] they adapted the path of charity and largesse and lending a helping hand to the desolate, and no one ever pursued foppery; rather, foppery was deemed to be becoming of women and a disgrace to men.

We have not yet forgotten the sheer number of such righteous men in every town who, without any external adornment, enjoyed all manners of respect among the people and many of the quarrels and disputes were resolved with the succour of these [men].

But according to Europism, as we evidently see, the basis of [a person's] respectability is foppery and having access to fêtes of hedonism. Righteousness and beneficence are not worth a nickel and every individual, whether a man or a woman, should amass money in any way possible and adorn themselves head to toe and attend dance parties and theatres and cinemas and soirées. This is why thievery and deceit are increasing daily and if we do not abandon this path [of Europism], these [traits] will be increasing constantly.

Thus, he who did not deem righteousness and beneficence to be suitable for Iranians [any longer] and [instead] wished them to become Europeanized in every respect, it would be good if he revealed his intent so that Iranians could make an informed and measured decision in accepting or rejecting his wish.[29]

Alas the world has stooped to such indecency and humankind has become so degenerate! A group of greedy Europeans have ruined their fellow compatriots

---

[29] Reference to Hasan Taqizadeh. See note 16 in Chapter 10 above.

[by exploiting them], and even so the fangs of their greed seek more blood so that now they have turned their voracious eyes to Asia. At a time like this, a group of Asians themselves have risen and do their utmost to assist these avaricious [Europeans] with their intent, bringing about the downfall of their own compatriots and on this path they even resort to lies and deception. Woe to this state [of affairs]! Pity on this state!

Chapter Sixteen

We must refrain from looking to Europe

They will ask, then what is to be done? We say that we must refrain from looking to Europe and return to the ancient ways of the East.

[Eastern] governments have no choice but to be uneasy about Europe and mindful of the Europeans' intentions about the East so that they can protect their countries, acquiring from Europe the latest arms or anything useful in administering a state and also essential principles and regulations in this regard.*

But the people must take their eyes off Europe. That today everyone including women and men and young and old have become conscious of Europe, emulating Europeans from dressing to eating to the entire realm of habits and ethics; [that they] take pride in associating with Europeans, considering worthier and superior those who are informed about their ways of life; [that they] pursue with interest whatever utterance they find spoken by a European, spreading utterances that are closer to delirium than to wisdom from some German man or some American woman; [that they] celebrate the adventures of famous Western men and women in every gathering, publicizing these stories by exaggerating any virtue they might find in them; [that] certain shameless people take the advancement of sciences in the West [as a means to] not sparing the people of the East from derision and reproach – all of these are symptoms of the malady of Europism which the East is infected with thanks to a handful of Western advocates.

---

* Similar to the law that was enacted in Iran in regard to trade with Europe last year. [Translator's note: The Foreign Trade Monopoly Bill (Qānun-e Enhesār-e Tejārat-e Khāreji) was introduced in the Consultative Assembly on 13 February 1931 and ratified on 25 February 1931. According to this law, foreign trade, whether import or export, became the state's monopoly. One of the stated goals of this law was to 'support and promote national industries'. Shadi Marefati, 'Qānun-e Enhesār-e Tejārat-e Khāreji', *Tejārat-e Fardā*, no. 62 (Mehr 1392/September 2013).]

As we have said, Europe is adrift in the desert of aberration and the path it has set foot on leads to a maelstrom, and the East, which has abandoned its own path and followed that caravan gone astray, is walking itself to destruction and must return from where it is now. It must return because its deliverance is in returning. It must return and rediscover those worthy things which it has abandoned and trampled upon. It must return and resume its own ancient ways of life.

We cannot do justice to Europe's deviation and its dark future. Even in an anarchic city where no one has ever heard of justice or humanity, even in such a place there will not be as much disarray as there is in today's Europe. And it will not be a surprise for this Europe to have the most alarming future.

Is it conceivable that in every town hoards of people are deprived of any kind of basic rights to life while those who have driven them to this state lift their heads in pride and boast of superiority in the world? [Is it conceivable that] a certain group of so-called learned men rise and declare the downtrodden group to be deserving of annihilation,[30] in this way tarnishing the image of science and humanity?!

Would it be a surprise if Europe falls, in retribution for this chaos and inhumanity, such that it won't rise from its ashes for centuries?!

In this state of affairs why is it that we have joined Europe, entangling ourselves in their errors?! Why is it that we have abandoned our own reliable and unperturbed way of life and taken the harmful and frightening path of others?!

Considering untruthfulness and fraud a disgrace; considering charity, hospitality, assisting strangers, aiding the desolate, and empathizing with kinfolk and neighbours as one's duty; considering the material world inferior; being concerned about and differentiating between righteous and sinful action in one's profession or trade; being humble and modest; the affluent feeling empathy with the poor; the poor shutting the eye of greed on the possessions of the affluent; and other virtues like these which have adorned our Eastern way of life are the fruits borne out of the seeds which the select of God [i.e. prophets] have planted and which the wise and the learned in each age have endeavoured

---

[30] Here Kasravi is most likely alluding to philosophers who espoused social Darwinism, such as Herbert Spencer and Walter Bagehot in the United Kingdom and William Graham Sumner in the United States.

to cultivate. Otherwise humanity, in its primitive stages of life, was in a similar state to millions of Europeans today.

Greeding after material possessions, not refraining from any misdeed in obtaining them and not sparing anyone from friend and foe [in obtaining more possessions] which are the prescribed Western ways of life were also the principles by which primitive nomads and early settler civilizations lived. However, since living in this way does not befit humans but brutes, God's select rose and endeavoured steadfastly to educate the world so that humans abandon such reprehensible dispositions, ordering [humans] to those blessed manners in the name of educating humanity – blessed manners each of which is the cause of the world's greatness and welfare and which anyone desiring goodness and happiness for humanity must strive to disseminate.

Now is it not a folly for us to abandon our ways of life with such adornments [as described above] and adopt the Western way of life, a way of life which is a stain on humanity's countenance?

We are not claiming that the people of the East and West are different or that Europeans are innately ignoble. Never! Europe was also similar to the East until in the past few centuries it attained certain inventions – inventions which it applauds and boasts of. But the truth is that these innovations are the cause of the world's destruction in that [these innovations] disproportionally elevate the status of certain groups while degrading the status of many others, and as a result of these disproportionate excesses the balance of life is disrupted. Just as people with vastly different body sizes cannot cohabit, excessive differences in possessions lead to a similar situation. But Europe is foolishly unaware of the ruination [effected] by this situation. Not only that, certain groups [among them], vainly deluded by these inventions, have risen against God and religion and have elevated evil over goodness with their absurd reasoning. The sum of these developments has led to Europe's plight, a predicament whose remedy will not be facile.

But the East, even though it has taken some strides towards Europism, is not yet fully entangled like Europe and can still return from the mid-way and erect a wall between [itself] and the West and peacefully attend to [its] own affairs.

Today fervent and informed men must endeavour to direct the masses away from this dangerous and ruinous path [of following Europe]. These zealots must be aware that Europism is invested in deceitfulness and that one can untangle the threads of deceitfulness with ease.

Only if we do not shun honesty can it be said that on this path to Europism one of the things we have cast to the ground and trampled upon is wisdom. A case in point is that the majority of the inhabitants of Zangān, Sushtar, Shiraz[31] or other small towns in Iran consider lies and dishonesty a disgrace, austerely abstain [from such deeds], observe righteous behaviour, and annually spend part of their wages or their trade's profits on [upholding] these principles. Meanwhile, a majority of the inhabitants of [the capital] Tehran, especially schooled youths, have based their lives on boldness and audacity and do not shun any manner of indecency, while being incognizant of all else except amassing wealth, self-beautification, and self-indulgence. From the perspective of Europism, these Tehranis are superior and worthier than those inhabitants of Zangān and every attempt is made to transform the latter into the former. Is this not folly?!

If there were any trace of wisdom, [they would see that] the inhabitant of Zangān is a human being, a worthy human being. But these [Europists], who have no other commitment except to their own pleasure and whims, are no different than cattle, than even beasts. Woe to Iran if someday all Iranians turn into such people.

If there were any trace of wisdom, who would elect external adornment over internal refinement and consider self-beautification the cause of honour and respect?! Who would insist so much upon Europism without having learned from Europe's predicament?!

It is a curiosity that many Euro-enthusiasts when they cannot deny the increasing competition and hardship in daily life and devaluation of good manners among the masses on this path [of Europism], they justify it by arguing that these are the signs of civilizational progress: more challenging life and more reprehensible traits among people. However, this justification is abundantly foolish and is exactly similar to a situation in which a man who has planted a sapling in his garden speaks to his offspring and neighbours of the tree's excellent breed and praises the sweetness of its fruits. But that

---

[31] Zanjān is a city in northwest Iran. Kasravi replaces the *j* in 'Zanjān' with a *g* in his usual style and in an attempt to Persianize the word. Shushtar is a city in southwestern Iran. Shiraz, the capital of the Fars province, is a culturally and historically important city in south-central Iran.

sapling grows into a fruitful tree, yielding bitter and disagreeable fruits that extinguish those who eat them. Even so, the man challenges [the evident] with the justification that the more bitter and disagreeable a tree's fruit, the more superior its breed is; and that this tree is so excellent that eating its fruits will ruin the eater!

We have said this repeatedly and will say it again: there is no good in the world if not for the people's welfare. And whatever is the cause of distress among people, it is [also] the cause of the world's degradation. It is the same with this movement of Europism: as our life has become more laborious, we have proportionally regressed.

Others have imagined that since Europe is powerful we must follow it, and whatever the consequences, we can also hope for the remedy from Europe itself. But this thought is also abundantly idiotic, for neither is Europe powerful nor must one follow whoever is in possession of power.

As we have said, from the perspective of [what constitutes] benefit and harm, the world of Europe is but [akin to] a master blacksmith because its achievement does not go beyond manufacturing innovative tools and making them available to the public. Let us now suppose that in a certain city a blacksmith has built impressive iron tools such that the townspeople are astounded by his artistry and purchase these tools at hefty prices. He has won fame in this way and has amassed enormous wealth. But his existence is reprehensible, for he has elevated a few of his children and has immersed them in opulence while at the same time uprooting his other children and relatives. Not only that, he has built and given to his [chosen] children instruments with which to annihilate the others. And his inhuman baseness is such that he does not care for the community except for [its utility for] his trade, and if need be he will uproot many a family in order to fill his treasure chest with gold and silver.

Is such a person powerful? If the townspeople follow him in his ways and habits after his demise, is this not a sign of their ignorance?!

Certainly if Europe displayed awareness and knowledge of what is harmful or beneficial for the world as it has displayed achievement in discovery and invention; or if some worthy figures had risen from there to lead the world, then it would not be wrong for the East or other parts of the world to follow Europe in ways of life. But now that Europe itself is entangled [in difficulty] beyond rescue, is it still proper that others follow it and share its plight?

If by 'powerful' is meant the might of the army in war, how can one be worthy of leadership as a result of such power?

If someone's neighbour were aggressive and carried a weapon, must one learn the ways of life from him?! Even though considering Europe as powerful in this sense is not accurate either. Today Europe is akin to an ancient and robust tree which looks immovable and mighty on the outside but is decayed and fragile on the inside and may at any time break and fall. Today Europe's only power and strength is from wielding deceptions and lies through a bunch of Euro-enthusiasts. Only by thinking of ways to deal with these enthusiasts can we find repose from Europe's harm.

Chapter Seventeen

What is religion?

We reiterate: the source of worldly prosperity is religion.

Those who show hostility to religion are either simpletons who cannot distinguish good from bad or lunatics who desire the world's destruction.

What has made humans the chosen ones among other creatures is religion. And those who abandon religion are the same as cattle or wild beasts that adorn themselves with exquisite attire.

We witness with our own eyes that despite acquiring immense knowledge and binding the earth to the heavens with its artistry, Europe has turned the world into an inferno for itself on account of irreligiosity such that in every corner millions suffer the harshest torment like the residents of hell. We witness those in Iran or other Eastern cities who have abandoned religion following the Europeans are, despite their adorned appearance, among the most contemptible of persons who have no other art except thievery and pillage and others draw no benefit from associating with them except suffering and harm.

Let us now advise what religion is. We recoil from any religion that separates humans from each other, advantaging one group over the others. We abhor any religion that is the cause of strife and bloodshed. We are referring to the religion in which humans enjoy fraternity and equality and in which no one seeks advantage over others, a religion in which the more charitable individuals are, the more valued they will be and in which outer adornment does not earn one worth or station. We are referring to the religion in which humans resist greed and heed others' benefit and loss in their dealings and trade. We are referring to the religion in which everyone considers it his duty to assist the desolate and to be mindful of his neighbours' and relatives' state. We are referring to the religion in which the affluent are concerned about the poor and the poor tolerate difficulties without coveting the wealth of the affluent. We are referring to the religion in which humans consider thievery and fraud a disgrace and not take pride in the riches which they have acquired through theft and dishonesty. We are referring to the religion in which humans judge themselves superior to animals, consider as their duty more than simply eating, sleeping, and indulging in self-gratification, and not torment each other like wild beasts.

If we imagine religion to be a house, its [foundational] four walls are knowledge of God, faith in the immortality of the soul, belief in the invisible world, and truthfulness and honesty. And good deeds are the embellishment of this house.

We all know God exists but we do not know what it is. It is in vain that some deny [His existence] and some seek [Him] with rational thought.

In regard to the soul, one must be cognizant that besides the living body which all living things possess, humankind is also in possession of an essence particular to him, and it is this essence which we call the soul. And we are certain that it lives on independently and eternally after the death of the living body and will receive reward or punishment for acts of goodness or evil committed in this world.

Those who consider humans to be the same as other animals and nothing beyond a living body have gone astray because humans are in possession of rationality and have perceptions which animals do not possess.

This is why humans find joy in doing good to others even if it may be to their own detriment or feel remorse for hurting others. But animals are deprived of such perceptions.

We also observe that while asleep, during which the living body is in a state of inertia, we perceive pleasures which cannot exist in a waking state. Likewise, it is in sleep that we feel very repentant about injustices [we have done] to the wretched, as a result of which we become so anxious that such anxiety is not possible in a waking state. It is evident from this [observation] that when the soul separates from the living body, it finds endless joy in good deeds while feeling so apprehensive about evil deeds that it cannot be captured in words. This in itself is retribution for its actions in this world; who knows what other retribution awaits.

As for the other two pillars of religion: [they are] honesty, not tainting the tongue with lies, not deceiving others, being the same inside and out; and integrity, recoiling the hand [of invasion] from the property and lives of people, not hurting others either with the hand or with the tongue, not wishing on others what one does not wish on himself. Honesty and integrity are the laws of humanism,[32] two attributes which every individual must be in possession of.

Rather, it must be said that lies and dishonesty are [a form of] madness or illness by which humans become afflicted because humanity never needs these indecencies for survival, for there is no benefit resulting from these but harm. When a group [of people] lives by honesty and integrity, not only do they fulfil their religious duty but they will also experience joy.

Those who do not abstain from lies and deceitfulness are extremely ignorant, afflicting themselves and others with trouble, because the person who finds gain in his lie and deceitfulness today will tomorrow receive harm from someone else's lie and deceitfulness. The person who unjustly takes someone's possession today, another oppressor will take his possession tomorrow. In this way everyone is afflicted and everyone is harmed.

This is the state of the world today: lives are wasted by deceiving and being deceived and oppressing and being oppressed while there is no repose or contentment except in words and labels.

All the struggles and suffering of individuals, the uncertainties, the anguish, afflictions, the quarrels and wars are the result of lies and dishonesty. If a group [of people] bases their lives on honesty and integrity, all these tribulations will leave from their midst and serenity and bliss will take their place.

In other words, as we have said, the cause of the world's problems is humans' clash with each other, and the instruments of this calamity are nothing but lies and dishonesty. If these indecencies cease to be, the world will find repose from harm and entanglement.

---

[32] The term 'humanism' has been used, here and elsewhere, as an equivalent to Kasravi's coinage 'ādami-gari'. As deployed by Kasravi, humanism should not necessarily be read in its Western philosophical sense of the individual as a secular, rational being with agency and a universal nature. Kasravi's usage conveys 'the practice of' being human, and humane, in a moral and commonsensical way. In this sense, Kasravi's 'ādami-gari' does coincide with the ethos of humanitarianism as a belief system involving practices such as the emphasis on the value of human life, benevolence and charity to reduce suffering and improve the conditions of human life.

Some might argue that lies and dishonesty are [part of] human nature so there is no cure for this ailment. But this idea is categorically false because those who have dishonesty in their nature are few in number, just as honesty and integrity does exist but in the natures of a few. The majority of the people are those who can be both honest or dishonest, and when they have a virtuous leader, they will not take but the path of honesty and integrity.

This is because in the bygone centuries whenever religion thrived and virtuous guides were among [the masses], scores of people tended towards goodness and there was not much thievery or fraud. Here in Iran it was common for a long time that people would not lock the doors of their houses or shops and robbery did not occur very often. Even today in many small hamlets the doors of houses and gardens are open and there is less robbery than in big cities even in the absence of police and watchmen.

Read the histories of the prophets and see for yourselves how in their time a great many people sought good deeds and considered lies and dishonesty a disgrace, a disgrace from which they distanced themselves by many miles.

The fact that today lies and deceitfulness have great currency and some think that survival is not possible without [committing] these indecencies is because Europe does not consider these reprehensible practices a disgrace.

In addition, [Europe] devalues honesty and deems beautified appearances to be the basis of high esteem. On the other hand, every day [Europe] creates more 'necessities' for life whose attainment drives people to [commit] more thievery and fraud. As a result of this, the world is moving towards baseness and every moment people's dishonesty will increase, unless they abandon this path and tread another one.

Regarding good deeds, in addition to recognition of God, faith in the invisible world, and honesty and integrity on which the edifice of religion is secured, the faithful must adorn that edifice with their good deeds. They must not withhold support and kindness from each other; every individual must be concerned with [the welfare of] his relatives and neighbours, and every individual must assist the downtrodden.

The affluent must always think of the desolate and must not withhold [assistance in the form of] loans from those who need it. They must know that a person's worth and value is his good deeds and whoever is more virtuous and charitable has a higher worth and station in this world and a more gleeful and happier soul in the next.

In sum: a faithful [person] is he who recognizes God and is not a stranger to Him in his affairs; believes in the eternity of the soul, knowing that whatever he does in this world from good or bad will receive reward or punishment in the next world; adopts a policy of honesty and integrity, avoiding lies and dishonesty even if there is hope of gain in them; and considers all humans, from any clime or any essence, to be brothers and does not withhold his charity or support [from them].

The more individuals with these qualities there are, the more prosperous the world and the more content the people of the world will be. If some people truly desire the world's improvement and its inhabitants' happiness (but have not, like the Europeans, made these words instruments of public deception), then they must perforce endeavour to spread religion.

Humanity can boast about [its] superiority and ascendancy and hold its head up only when this [brand of] religion has spread to every place and the root of irreligiosity has shrivelled from the world. It is on that day that contentment will extend to every nation.

Chapter Eighteen

Religion is humanism

Many Europeans do not consider humans separate from animals and in their view humans can, indeed must, live like wild beasts and animals. This is an example of Europeans' unsound judgment.

Humanity is akin to animals as a living organism and [subsequently] there are some animal dispositions apparent in humans. Greed, which the Europeans have adopted as a principle in their lives, is nothing but a bestial disposition. Theft, stealing others' possessions, and harming the weak is the disposition of wild beasts. Lack of compassion towards one's own kind is the disposition of all animals.

Even so, humanity cannot be counted among other animals because humans possess soul and rationality and are capable of perceptions which other animals do not possess.

What must be said is that humans are the chosen ones among other creatures [only] if they have faith in religion, resist greed, consider all humans as equal and brothers, wish a good life upon all, consider lies and dishonesty a disgrace, and do not withhold their assistance to the downtrodden and the powerless. The comparison between such humans and beasts is the same as the comparison between millstone and rubies: although both are of the same breed [i.e. stones], they are vastly different in value and worth.

However, the individual who knows nothing of life except eating and sleeping and self-indulgence, who does not resist greed and wants the world for himself and never worries about the poor, such a person is not different from beasts and cattle; pity if the word human is applied to him.

What difference is there between those individuals who seek others' ruin for wealth and want, and canines gathering around a corpse and fighting each other? What is the difference between those individuals who utterly ruin many families with the might of machines as they boast of their achievement, and the wild beasts that kill the weak among their own kind, roaring triumphantly as they roll them in blood and dirt? Those persons who engage in robbery and stealing others' possessions, how are they superior to foxes and hyenas? Those who have no empathy for the misery and troubles of their own kind, how are they better than the sheep that calmly grazes next to another sheep's carcass? Those who have erected twenty and thirty-story edifices without caring about the homeless men and women next to their walls, how can they have a share of humanism? Those who consider life to be about eating, sleeping and self-indulgence, how are these people different from bovine like oxen and mules?

Humanity must take wisdom as its guide and drive animalism away from itself. They must set aside greed which is the most despicable of dispositions, because the world belongs to all its inhabitants and each has a share in it in accordance with his daily portion. They must know that those who cohabit in the same city or on the same land next to each other must vigilantly refrain from deceiving or lying to one another; otherwise they will all be trapped and deprived of repose. They must know that they are not akin to animals that vanish out of existence after death, but that their soul remains eternally and will be remorseful of evil deeds in this world, a remorse that cannot be captured in words.

Indeed, religion asks no more of humans than inclination towards the ethos of humanity. In other words, because humans live together in the same communities, this living condition calls for each individual being committed not only to his own welfare but also to public welfare. They must consider lying and dishonesty, which are the root of the community's problems, as absolute folly and hold liars and fraudsters in contempt.

Each community must imagine its own city, even the whole world, to be a house where all should live like relatives and brothers.

This is the ethos of humanity. This is also what is called civility or civilization because it is with this type of behaviour that humans can come together and render life's hardships easy with each other's backing.

Those who cannot behave accordingly, they should at least follow [the behaviour of] oxen and sheep and refrain from hurting or harassing each other. If they don't give each other any benefit, at least they don't hurt each other [either]. If they are devoid of the ethos of humanity and civility, at least they can live like cattle.

Those who cannot even do this and cannot live except by hurting and harassing each other, these are not humans but brutes clothed in human garb. The convergence of these people in the same place not only yields no benefit but also produces all manners of harm. So much the better for this group to live apart from each other like lions and leopards.

This is why the world of Europe today is the world of wild beasts because the basis of life [there] is domination such that in every corner a powerful group has debilitated a vast number of the powerless, constricting their livelihoods and bragging, like lions and leopards, about their own victory in this encounter and about their superiority and dominance. Meanwhile the hungry roam the streets in search of meat and bread like wolves attacking livestock. Many others obtain daily bread through theft, like foxes and hyenas, or else raid caravans on the highway like wolves. Where is there a trace of humanity in this world?

Europe enumerates its achievements: ascending to the skies, descending to the bottom of seas, hearing sounds from a hundred miles away [i.e. telephone], electrical lamps, steam engines, and the like. Each of these is an achievement. But what use [is there] in them if humanity cannot order its affairs wisely and if humanity's share of peace and repose from all these sciences and achievements is less than cattle and if its treatment of its own kind is worse than predators?

Instead of all these achievements, it would be better for Europe to think of a remedy to deliver itself from this type of life which only befits fierce predators.

It must be said without reservation: the condition of Europe today – which it insists on tainting Asia and other regions with as well – is the most reprehensible state. For as long as the world has existed, it has not witnessed such calamity, and since the day it has come into existence, humanity has not been cursed with such baseness. Humanity did not even experience such a state during the era of Bedouinism and nomadism in the ancient times because even though at that time the basis of survival was also brute force and dominance, every powerful person not sparing the powerless any mischief, at that time human interdependence and mutual need was not as pronounced as [it is] today: a powerless person could free himself of oppression by fleeing to a new place. But today the powerless have no way out except death.

Only if we do not fear honesty can it be said that Europe has abandoned wisdom and reason and its actions are nothing but madness. No doubt the path Europe has taken is but to destruction, and even though signs of destruction are apparent from every corner, Europe is never remorseful of its actions and is foolishly engaged in flying to the sky and plunging into the bottom of the sea and other futile activities which have no benefit to the world's tranquillity.

[Europe is] like an illusionist who lets out his children, hungry and bare, on the street and when the neighbours reproach and question him, he begins to enumerate his achievements: I ascend to the sky, descend into the sea and resurface unharmed, I can hear sound from a hundred miles away. Is this action and this response not the sign of the man's madness?!

Another sign of Europe's madness is the design the socialists have for the world: that the freedom of labour and trade be taken away so that all are equal and there are no affluent or poor people.

Do the Europeans think the world has just appeared or that humans have just come into existence that they can devise new plans for it all the time? Hundreds of centuries have passed on this earth and humans have had civic existence since the ancient times and lived happily and leisurely. So what need is there for the Europeans to devise new paths for the world to tread?

This idea is exceedingly raw and infantile because just as humans are not created equally, they cannot be equal in life. Each person must benefit from life's pleasures in accordance with his and his clan's capability.

What must be prevented is lies and dishonesty since lying and deceitfulness have disrupted that divine order, making way for those who benefit beyond their capability and endeavour. If some genuinely desire the world's welfare, they must cherish religion, the guardian of humans against lying and deceit, and make its reign over the world supreme. It is only thus that not only life's many ups and downs will be limited, but also labour and trade will be free so that humans' talents are not wasted.

However, in Europe besides lying and dishonesty, the other adversity is machinism which has disrupted life's balance and created excessive ups and downs [in life]. The socialists are also irritated with machinism, but rather than channelling their hostility towards the machine, they disrupt the tried and true order of millennia [by attempting to create a new social order].

From these arguments the East must come to itself and understand Europe as it is and not be deceived by a handful of Euro-enthusiasts. They [people of the East] must be certain that they will reap no benefit from Europism except remorse. It is in vain that they reject their own peaceful and honourable way of life.

The Easterners must know that before long anarchy will arise in Europe and for years, perhaps centuries, there will reign nothing but upheaval in that region. If today Easterners preserve their ancient ways of life, at that time they will not only live in peace but they will also be able to offer assistance and guidance to Europe.

The end of part one of *Ethos*.

Ethos: Book Two

Chapter One

In God's immaculate name

Oh Lord, I commence in thy name and seek thy assistance. Make this path facile to me and help me overcome the obstacles. Thy servants' hearts are in thy hands. Arouse good men to my aid and upright men in my support. Make ears open and hearts receptive to my words.

Oh Lord, what grave times, what a turbulent world! Some have abandoned the path of salvation and are entrapped in the desert of deviance. Instead of delivering themselves, they wish others to be trapped as well, calling everyone to themselves. The world has abandoned peace and freedom, walking on their own feet towards the trap.

Alas this perversion, woe to this menace.

Oh Westerners, oh you who consider yourselves better and prevail over others, alas you do not recognize your own faults. You boast about your superiority but forget the damage you have inflicted upon the world. Your false indoctrinations have disrupted the world's order and tarnished the face of humanity. It is in vain that you boast of superiority and ascendancy. The path you are walking is towards destruction. Strange that you also call others to it. You are entangled yourselves and wish to entrap others as well. This grudge and bloodthirstiness and deceit is not befitting of humans. A life of coercion and deception does not befit humans but wild beasts.

You advance rapidly on the path of manufacturing machines but have abandoned peace and contentment which is the world's singular desire. You have stirred the world into motion, but where is the benefit in this motion? 'Thou hast dug out the wall's foundation yet overlay the roof'.[1] You drink poison out of a golden cup. You sleep hungry in a crystalline mansion.

---

[1] This saying refers to the futile act of mending the surface of something, such as a building, while the foundation is faulty. Kasravi uses a slightly modified version of the verse by the eleventh-century Persian poet, Sanā'i Ghaznavi: 'The king that seizeth his treasury from the peasant / [Is like he who] digeth out the wall's foundation yet overlayeth the roof'. Also see note above on Sa'di in Book 1:6.

Oh you Easterners, you, including men and women, who are stirred into motion and hasten towards Europism and on this path have abandoned all your possessions from religion to humanism and contentment, you have incurred a tremendous loss. You have not assessed the bad and good in this movement [of Europism] and do not distinguish between benefit and loss. You have been enamoured with the West's wizardry and think that all the Westerners' ways are equally fantastical and special, taking this path [to Europism] on the basis of this false illusion.

Brothers and sisters, hold back your haste a moment and ponder your action. Europism is nothing but a trap, a trap which one cannot escape for centuries, a calamity that one cannot find a recourse from with ease. Those who praise Europe are fools who cannot distinguish good from bad, or else vermin who wish the world to be troubled and misguided.

This world has been in existence for centuries. From your region have risen prophets who did not wish but for the welfare of the world, chosen ones who did not have but pure hearts in their bosoms, enlightening people with the ethos of humanity and making the path to salvation manifest. You are trampling upon that ethos and deviating from the path of salvation.

Your story is akin to the story of the birds that see a bird perched next to grain and water [set as trap]. The birds hear its enchanting chirping from a distance and hasten towards it and become ensnared in the trap. Or the story of the villagers who live peacefully in their houses and gardens until one day they see the outlines of a group [of people] in the desert, a thick mass [of people] and their hustle and bustle working hard like bees in a hive. The villagers become intrigued and resolve to seek [the cause] until some return from the group with news [of the goings-on], tremendously good and wondrous news, exceedingly hyperbolic praises. The poor villagers lose their minds, relinquishing their houses and gardens, both men and women stirred into motion and taking the desert path towards that group. When they reach them, they find a group [of people] who have lost their way and are trapped in the desert of misguidance. One group [has divided] into sects, each sect thirsty for the others' blood; another group [are] artful illusionists but utterly deprived of wisdom and humanity; another group begrudging and deceitful; another group base their lives on coercion and domination such that no one is concerned about or heeds the others; another group is in such disarray that some [within the group] cannot keep up due to the [weight of] excess provisions they carry while others [within the same group] are lifeless due to lack of provisions.

What good will be the villagers' remorse, especially since there is no return to their houses and they will be entrapped in that manner?

You who abandon your peaceful existence, cast down and trample upon the precious treasures of the East, such as religion, humanity and admirable dispositions, hastening so [towards Europe] without knowing the aftermath of Europism – if you do not return from this path, you will have the same type of remorse [as the villagers].

You do not comprehend Europe as it is. Its achievements in manufacturing machinery and similar technologies have dazzled your eyes such that you do not recognize its defects, especially because some have given excessive praise to Europe, not sparing a single hyperbole, in order to deceive you. I will praise Europe as it is, illustrating each and every one of its achievements and deficiencies, so that you become aware of how you have been deluded and what a dreadful path you have chosen.

Chapter Two

How has Europe been entrapped?

Europe's troubles – which are leading it, with tied hands and feet, towards destruction – are phenomena that have appeared in the last two centuries and have intensified [since]. If we go back two hundred years, Europe has the status of other regions, the only thing disrupting the public's peace being the wars that erupt between states or rebellions occurring in this or that corner.

After some time (in the second half of the eighteenth century) inventions emerge, each invention leading to another until gradually mighty machines appear and factories are erected.

Certain individuals have been hostile to these inventions from the outset. But the majority of people consider these inventions as the cause of progress and ascendency in the world and celebrate [them]. Bands of people lose their autonomous trades or abandon them having no choice but to turn to factories. Even farmers abandon agriculture and pour onto the cities, accepting employment as workers in these factories.

From here the balance of life is upset. Certain individuals find quick and easy ways to accumulate wealth such that every day others' incomes plummet while adding to the former's wealth. Like a sieve that constantly shakes, straining some grains while holding a few large chunks on its surface, machines and factories also make a large group of people penniless every year and turn their possessions over to the industrialists.

Every year a series of new machines emerge, speedier than the aging machines, and in this way annually the number of the poor increases while the wealth of the capitalists grows.

In the meantime, the spirit of religion wanes in Europe because the masses had become fed up with the wickedness of the priests. The priests had used religion as a means to dominate the masses for centuries and did not withhold any manner of inhumanity. Religion, which is the basis of virtue and altruism, had in the hands of these rascals turned into a means for oppression and vice. This is why in France and other regions, when the masses rebel against the monarchs and oppressors, they also rise up against the priesthood. And since the masses did not know any religion except what had been conveyed to them by the priests, they start to become antagonistic to religion.

Like the dumb sheep who upon growing horns seeks freedom from the shepherd, testing its horn fighting against him before all else, the industrialists of the West also tussled with religion from the outset. Like a blacksmith who claims to be a physician or boasts about his legislative [skills], these industrialists, too, meddle in all affairs, conceited by their industrialism and machinery. They have mostly been inclined towards disrupting everything that has come down [to us] from ancient times, disputing even God and religion.

If irreligiosity were limited to lack of knowledge of God, I would not address it [here] because God is free from this need [to be known]. However, irreligiosity is always followed by immense loss. It is as a result of this [irreligiosity] that in Europe individuals known as scientists or philosophers have emerged and, as if hostile to the human species and resentful of its ascendency over beasts and cattle, have risen in hostility against that ascendancy with the aid of a series of poisonous claims. The singular wish of these perpetrators of harmful thoughts is for humans not to consider themselves different from cattle and beasts and to seek nothing but their [animalistic] ways. This harmful indoctrination is one of the reasons behind the West's problems, and it is one of the curses upon Europe that such philosophers have emerged.[2]

One of the inherent qualities in animals, especially in predators, is 'greed'. A camel carcass can feed several leopards, and yet a leopard tends to possessively take all of it, driving away the others. This disposition is also in human nature. And because this is a reprehensible quality, harming both the

---

[2] Social Darwinism, also referenced briefly in Book 1:15, reemerges here as one of the underlying themes in this chapter. According to the tenets of social Darwinism, the evolutionary concepts of survival of the fittest and natural selection are said to apply to various fields in the social sciences including history and economics. The views of its most influential figure, Herbert Spencer (1820–1903), have been used to justify laissez-faire capitalism, imperialism, scientific racism and economic determinism, from its inception in the nineteenth century through to the twenty-first century. Repeated instances of the neoliberal motto 'there is no alternative' upheld by various leaders from Augusto Pinochet to Margaret Thatcher and Ronald Reagan, for example, has sometimes been linked to the evolution of social Darwinism within the neoliberal order. See, for instance, George Monbiot, *How Did We Get into This Mess?: Politics, Equality, Nature* (London: Verso, 2016).

world and the greedy alike, prophets and dignitaries who sought the world's welfare ardently opposed this disposition and endeavoured to annihilate it.

However, in Europe this reprehensible bestial quality has been promoted among humans due to, on the one hand, the emergence of factories which have made accumulation of wealth quick and easy and, on the other, the false indoctrinations of those [aforementioned] philosophers. This is why accumulation of wealth and amassing money which were [deemed] vile in the olden times are at this time highly desirable. And for thousands of individuals belonging to [the strata of] the wealthy and the captains of industry, despite having hoarded millions, the furnace of their greed is still flaring up, from whose blaze the livelihood of hundreds of families turns to dust.

What is worse is that Europe adds coercion, deception and other vices to this issue [i.e. greed]. Previously, Europe had learned to endorse all manners of wickedness in the field of politics,[3] not fearing anyone or anything nor troubling itself with [the loss of] people's lives or the prosperity of towns and villages. Today some employ this catastrophic principle in the accumulation of wealth as well.

Furthermore, as a result of disruption in the order of life, increase in the [number of] poor and workers, the spread of greed, and the capitalists' and the wealthy's lack of compassion for the desolate, [political] parties have emerged and vicious factionalism and hostility between the two groups ensues. The wealthy and the poor who had previously had a brotherly coexistence now rally against each other, attempting to displace and uproot one another.

The poor consider the wealthy as thieves and their possessions as stolen wealth, setting as their ultimate goal the annihilation of the latter. The wealthy, for their part, do their best to tighten their grip on the livelihoods of the former and view them as deserving of extinction due to their powerlessness.

In addition, the proliferation of machines and factories which mass-produce all manners of goods and export them to other countries, especially to the distant lands of the East, floods the factories with capital, bringing excessive profit to the [producing] country. These profits are appealing to governments; every government thus seeks to erect more factories operating longer hours in each city. To make this possible, governments support businessmen and

---

[3] A likely early reference to Machiavellianism which Kasravi returns to both in the following chapter and again in Book 2: 6.

owners of capital. Out of all of this arises new rivalries among countries, adding one more layer to ancient grudges [among them]. And since excessive production must have access to ever greater markets, Western governments inevitably turn their gaze towards Eastern cities. We all know what manner of predatory inhumanity is permitted by any [Western] government that seeks to lay its hand on a corner of the East, not even stopping at war and bloodshed over securing more markets.

In the hands of these [states], trade and commerce, which are a means of providing welfare for people, become pretexts for war, oppression and injustice. All the havoc which the Europeans have wreaked in the East has been for the purpose of profiteering.

On the other hand, the governments' support for mechanical production has contributed to an increase in new machinery and inventions, leading to even greater proliferation [of machines]. For a long time the harm of machines was [limited to] people losing their traditional means of sustenance and trade and having to settle for much lower wages in factories. But an even more injurious harm will ensue. Settling for lower wages represents the still-unripe fruits of machines. After a while, those fruits will ripen into a situation in which hordes of workers will be laid off and lose their source of subsistence: hunger, misery, black death – these have been the fruits of machines!

Today in every corner there are scores of unemployed people without any remedy for their misery – the poor left without a helping hand. This is Europe's predicament, which if not addressed will drive all of the West towards destruction. We will discuss each [of Europe's predicaments] one by one separately so that Easterners can comprehend the true meaning of Europism.

Chapter Three

Ancient grudges

The animosity among the peoples of Europe is the result of the wars among them in the previous centuries, such as the wars between France and England, Germany and France, Austria and Germany, France and Italy, Russia and the Ottoman [Empire] and the like which are well known in histories.

Centuries have passed without [anyone] conceiving of a remedy. If instead of progress in technology and industry Europe had progressed in understanding [what is of] benefit or harm to the world and conceived of a remedy for these animosities, it would be a hundred times better and more beneficial.

It has been well said that the European flies in the sky like a bird and pierces through water like fish but on land he cannot live like humans. Behold how the people whose claim to superiority and dominance has filled the world treat each other on the pretext of resentment and hostility.

European patriotism, which enjoys so much fame, is itself the fruit of these hostilities. One group loathes the others so much that they thirst for their blood, and when there is a call to war, most people rush to the field voluntarily so that they can dip their hands in the enemy's blood. They have called animosity and bloodthirstiness patriotism. Fortunate [are] those who present their misdeeds in the garb of goodwill!

When the two groups engage in conflict and war becomes frequent between them, they are both trapped and animosity teaches them all manners of inhumanity. These animosities and the bloodthirstiness have cost Europe itself dearly. It has been as a result of these that a new field known as politics has appeared where coercion, bloodshed, disruption of [genuine] improvements, lies, deception or any form of misconduct are permitted, a field in which one must exterminate the opponent without having concern for anyone or anything. Since some individuals have emerged out of this field triumphant and have achieved great feats, their name and fame have contributed more than anything to the promotion of this field such that today most of Europe's bright and observant men exert [themselves] on this path.

But these practices have tainted Europe's image and have afforded it a scandalous history. For centuries the people of the world will not forget these vices which Europe commits in the name of politics and will curse its name.

What is worse is that these vices have led to other misdeeds. Certain individuals also admit [the use of] coercion and deceit in party intrigues, patronage and accumulation of wealth. If something is inadmissible, it must be inadmissible everywhere. Since one can trample upon humanity in politics, one can also do the same in other areas.

This itself is a great loss to Europe, a loss that cannot be remedied for centuries.

This is no idle talk: reason has journeyed away from Europe. In a place where the foundation of life has been [erected upon] coercion and deceit for a long time, does reason not journey away from there? As the Europeans themselves say, what is not used loses its utility and tends to diminish.[4]

If reason is involved, why do the wise not congregate and devise a remedy for these animosities? Europe's problems are not extra-terrestrial events whose remedy is out of their own hands. If an assembly of wise men convenes and strives sincerely, all these troubles are remediable. But where is such an assembly [to be found]?!

Today if representatives from the peoples of Europe gather in one place, at such a meeting there will be none but hostility in [their] hearts and lies on [their] tongues. This is why their ailments cannot be cured.

We witnessed the war of 1914, what it was and how it engulfed [the world] in fire. Even so, did they take an example [from it]? Are they not contemplating another more destructive war? As they say themselves, they are sitting atop a volcano that is feared to erupt any moment.

Granted, a convention has been founded after that war [the First World War] to arbitrate among states and prevent war. Another association was also

---

[4] Reference here is to the Darwinian notion of 'vestigial' organs. Here Kasravi is applying the biological concept to his argument that Europe has lost its faculty of reason due to non-use.

founded three years ago to contain the use of instruments of war.[5] They sit and stand [at meetings], come and go, they have exhausted the world with their negotiations, but which powerful state is not fantasizing about preying on others? Or which one is genuinely intent on preventing war?

If there is no war, what will happen to those age-old grudges? How will the factories, erected with enormous capital for the purpose of manufacturing cannons and firearms and other instruments of homicide, sell [their goods] for millions?

If the Geneva Conventions for arbitration were erected on integrity, it would be the greatest and most beneficial organization in the world. Such a solution is a necessity for world peace and the prevention of war and massacre, but on the condition of integrity, on the condition of sincerity,* not for the powerful [states] to use it as a means to advance their own machinations.

If this great European association is not founded on deceit, why did they not prevent the war between China and Japan?[6] Could they not have forced Japan to abide by the Convention? Or could each state not have contributed forces to China's aid, or encourage one of the neighbouring states to do so? They could at least not have sold arms to Japan. But we witnessed how they even refrained from aiding China in this way, because they themselves are not sincere with each other and are fearful of one another. This is because they have gathered [at the Convention] to deceive one another, using the prevention of war as a pretext.

Another result of those belligerent hostilities is that since the advent of inventions, most of the inventions have served wars. The ingenious masters of Europe have also created machineries of homicide so that a single soldier can do the work of one hundred others. While war itself is a disgrace to the world, a form of madness contracted by humans, these masters have intensified its severity and destruction one hundred-fold. Even so, on the slightest excuse

---

[5] This is in reference to the Protocol for the Prohibition of the Use in War of Asphyxiating, Poisonous or Other Gases, and of Bacteriological Methods of Warfare (commonly known as the Geneva Protocol), which came into effect in February 1928.

* The Quran has also recommended this path in preventing armed conflict among Muslim clans: And should two factions among Believers go to war, make settlement between them. But should one of them maltreat the other, then fight against the oppressor until it returns to Allah's ordinance. [Kasravi's reference, cited in Arabic, is to Quran 49:9].

[6] Reference to the Japanese invasion of the Chinese province of Manchuria in 1931.

they rise against each other in war, engulfing all of Europe, rather the whole world, in fire. Praise be to [this] humanism!

There was a time when Europeans disapproved of guns and considered its use ignoble because it kills from a distance. Today they annihilate hundreds of people with bombs or gas and brag about it. The baseness of [today's] world can be measured from this.

Europeans exert as much effort on few other activities as they do on war. During war many learned men and even school teachers rush to the battlefield and taint their hands with their own kind's blood on the pretext of patriotism. However, while today thousands of families struggle with the disaster of unemployment, sinking in ruination, there is no one to offer a solution in the name of compatriotism.

Chapter Four

Scepticism and false indoctrination

In regard to scepticism I blame the priests again, not only the priests but also all their colleagues from any persuasion or creed. Not having comprehended God the Creator, each created a deity out of their own imagination and took Him to the churches, battlefields, coronations and to patients' bedsides.

Whatever is said about the damage they have done is appropriate. However, it is not appropriate for certain individuals to use these damages as a pretext to [completely] wash religion off their hands. If stinging serpents gather around a spring, must the thirsty relinquish that spring?! Why not crush the serpents' heads and alleviate their burning thirst with the help of that pure water?!

Europe must remove the priests from between itself and God and get closer to God, not to turn its back on God on account of resentment towards them [the priests]. Europe must know that religion is the ethos of humanity and whoever turns away from religion shall become bereft of humanity.

As we have said* the majority of people are those who can either find their way through advice and guidance or lose their way through deception and false teachings. This is why God has always chosen and sent guides and if we see with the eye of wisdom, human progress has been the result of nothing but the efforts of these chosen guides.

We know the nature of beasts: brute force, cruelty, greed, killing each other and the like. These dispositions have been amply common among humans as well, until the prophets rose to battle those [dispositions] and to cleanse masses of people of them. Even today in Iran and other Eastern regions a majority of people keep away from lying and double-dealing even if it is profitable for them; they consider hospitality, assistance to the downtrodden, and loaning to

---

* Book One, p. 54 [1:17].

the poor an obligation, and do so even if it comes at a loss to themselves. Are these [qualities] not the result of the prophets' efforts?!

However, in Europe once invention begins and religion loses its currency, some individuals begin to spread falsehood. They blurt out a series of poisonous claims, absurd and unfounded claims with no result other than misguiding the people. However, Europe calls these [claims] 'philosophy' and has spread them across the world.

We will call to mind one of these philosophies: a certain British person has some theories about the creation of the world and the manner in which humans and animals appeared which are known by his name. This person claims: creation is a battlefield in which creatures are in constant rivalry where the powerful eliminate the powerless for their own survival. Putting aside whatever the truth of these theories, some have extended them to human life. In their estimation, all humans are in a struggle and battle against each other and here, too, the powerful are allowed to ruin the powerless for their own benefit or deprive them of peace and well-being. Others have gone a step further and assert that the weak must be sterilized or annihilated so that humans become more robust with every new generation until after centuries a stronger race emerges.[7]

These claims which we call 'Darwinism' are today dispersed across the West and have found their way to the East too. And who knows what ills have risen out of this, especially conjoined with the trait of greed which is in human nature. These thoughts are to the greedy like petroleum [poured] on raging fire.

We witness how the British propose these notions in relation to India. The capitalists in Europe resort to such theories in relation to the unemployed and the desolate whom they have reduced to the most miserable state. Thousands in every city and town trample upon the ethos of humanity in their trade, using these principles in justification.

Just as a destroyer of towns can in a single day ruin improvements that take years in the making, these poisonous claims by Western philosophers have

---

[7] In the first part of this paragraph, Kasravi is obviously referring to Darwinism, to which he returns in the following paragraph. In the second part, he is referring to social Darwinism, which he has addressed in the previous pages. In the third part, he is referring to the ideology informing the practice of eugenics, selective breeding among humans with 'desirable' traits in order to 'improve' the human species. Eugenics would later become the ideology that propelled the Nazi state's 'scientific' experiments, but it also had powerful advocates elsewhere in Europe and the U.S.

wasted both the prophets' millennial efforts and ruined the foundations of humanity. Pity if the name 'philosopher' is applied to these [individuals]. Why not call them mad and consider their claims as nonsense and delirium?!

If it is permissible in human life for the powerful to debilitate and ruin the powerless, then what are all these laws for?! Why then do they dole out punishment to thieves and brigands?! Why then do they execute murderers?!

Though humans are of the same essence as animals, they are not the same as animals because the former possesses reason and must conform to reason in life. However, animals do not possess it [reason]. Reason is a torch entrusted to humans by the Creator so that they can tread [life's path] with ease. Reason is the heart's eye, and animals, which do not possess reason, are like the blind.

Thus, if humans abandon their reason and imitate cattle and beasts on orders from Western philosophers, it is similar to a person, in a dark night standing at a muddy road, who puts out the lamp he is carrying and instead treads in the dark, constantly slipping and muddying himself from head to toe. Or [it is similar to] the person with vision who, upon seeing the blind dragging their feet while walking and falling from one sinkhole to the next, blindfolds himself and walks, slipping and falling like the blind.

In regard to the sterilization or annihilation of the disabled, one must ask how is it determined who is disabled and who is abled? Or how can one separate the two groups from each other? And then what benefit ensues for humans from having more strength and being robust, especially if this end can be achieved only after the passage of thousands of years?[8] Is it deemed appropriate for humans to constantly shed blood and annihilate their own kind in the hopes of attaining a profitable end after thousands of years?!

It is a wonder that Westerners, on the one hand, insist on reducing humans to animals while on the other proclaim [human] progress and ascendancy around the world. In truth Europe has uprooted humanism with these principles and with those practices in politics, capitalism and party intrigues. The only difference between the practices of Westerners and the actions of beasts is that the beasts only know [how to use] brute force, and where this is not effective, they are left powerless. However, the

---

[8] In critiquing the senselessness of eugenics, here Kasravi invokes the Darwinian principle of 'descent with modification' according to which changes in a population will be visible after eons.

Europeans also benefit from knowing deception so that wherever coercion is not effective, they will use it [i.e. deception].

We are not asserting that all Europeans are similar in this manner. No doubt there are among them plenty of noble men who are not in agreement with these principles and practices and are grief-stricken like us. Europe has for centuries been the home of Christianity and despite all the vices of the priests, it cannot be said that religion has not borne any fruit or that its fruits have entirely been ruined. Such an assertion is impermissible. Besides, owing to the rebellions in France and other regions against the oppressors a century ago, a series of vastly beneficial and valuable ideas were kindled in the hearts of the Europeans, all of which has undoubtedly not disappeared. We never claim that sincerity has altogether left all of Europe. Everywhere our reference is to generalities in the population. These movements in irreligiosity, greed and deceitfulness, which have come into being since a century and a half ago and have been increasing daily, our reference is to these movements, as are our criticisms in this regard.

Chapter Five

The harms of the machine

I will write all I know about the machine. However, I am aware that some people will not easily accept these arguments. Even some among my friends who believe in me will resist [what I am about to say]. But I am firm in my assertions.

Europe says: machines reduce human suffering. Instead of a person weaving daily two pairs of socks, a machine weaves one hundred pairs in a day. Why would someone denounce such a useful instrument?

It is not reasonable to deny this benefit of the machine. However, the disservice, even the damages, that this apparatus has inflicted upon the world is also plenty. It must be said that if machines have reduced the hand-toils a hundred-fold, they have increased the heart-toils a thousand-fold. Further, this apparatus has created knots in human life that cannot easily be undone and there is a great fear that the thread will be torn [while trying to untie the knot].

The story of the inventions of Europe is the story of an ant that grows wings and perhaps these wings will be the cause of its ruin.

It takes a dedicated book to speak of machines. [Here] we only speak of manufacturing machines that have deprived craftsmen of their craft. The first detriment of these machines is that they disrupt the balance of life – a balance that is in place for the welfare of a community.

It is not just that in each factory hundreds or thousands of workers toil and each does not receive but a small wage while the fruit of their suffering remains with the factory owner. The point is also that most of the things these factories manufacture or weave, yielding a plentitude [of goods], are useless and unnecessary. However, because they [captains of industry] are dominant, they convince the masses to buy and use them and in this way snatch the people's money from them deceitfully and illegitimately.

Like a sieve that constantly shakes, straining some grains while holding a few large chunks on its surface, these machines also make hundreds or thousands of families penniless, gathering and turning their possessions over to a few individuals. Wherever these instruments become common, in a short while a peculiar upward and downward move occurs in the lives of the people where a few [individuals] will be greatly elevated [by amassing capital and possessions] while large groups [of people] will be considerably dragged down. Will the palace of happiness not collapse on such uneven ground?!

The mention of machines brings to my mind a violet-coloured blossom that grows in casaba melon fields. The ignorant consider it a flower and revel in its sight. But what burden of grief weighs on the poor farmer's heart by sighting it? [This is] because this harmful plant, though it has the appearance of a flower, is more harmful than thorn such that when it appears in a garden, in a short while it dries the melon bushes making their freshness and lustre wither away.

There is no forgiveness for this sin committed by the machine in assisting the greedy with a quick and easy way to amass wealth. Today in Europe one-third of the people are hired hands who have to work from dawn to dusk to earn daily sustenance. Pity that even such work is rare because thanks to the unrestrained increase in machines and their ever-increasing speed the ultimate result has been that millions of persons have lost their jobs, finding the means of providing for themselves and their families taken away. Today this is the greatest challenge for Europe.

European [news] agencies broadcast astonishing news last year:

In England and Germany and America the hungry organized a demonstration, travelling to the capitals. In Germany they had written on their signs: Food for our children. In New York there are three hundred thousand vagrant children. In Germany many committed suicide due to hunger. In Poland people commit crimes in order to be incarcerated so that they can be free from the anxiety over dying of hunger [i.e. receive free food in jail]; those whose jail term has come to an end will not leave out of fear of hunger.[9]

Are not these shameful for the world?! What is [the meaning of] hunger when there has been precipitation from the sky and crops have grown from

---

[9] Kasravi is referring to the dismal state of the economy during the Great Depression in the 1930s, leading to unprecedented unemployment, poverty, hunger and displacement.

the soil? When has there ever before been organized rallies and protest signs by the hungry?! Those who criticized their ancestors' feudalism, what do they call this state of hunger?! Is this the meaning of welfare promised by the machine?!

Another detriment of machines is that trade and commerce which used to be the answer to [the question of] public welfare – in this manner: some produce or weave or plant what people need while others transport and sell them from one town to the next – have today turned into problems for the world thanks to the emergence of machines.

As we said, bourgeois capitalists of Europe compel people to purchase whatever machines produce, and however much they produce, even though they [the people] may not need it. And because they are the dominant class, they achieve their goal through whatever means possible [i.e. through advertising]. This itself is a reprehensible innovation in the world's affairs.

The turmoil that exists in the world today and that has involved governments everywhere is the result of that innovation. The problem among families where men and women are not relieved a single day from anxiety over clothes and shoes is the result of that [innovation]. This self-beautification which has spread everywhere, men and women sacrificing self-restraint, humanity and honour for grooming their heads and bodies, is the result of that [innovation].

What is worse is that governments in Europe are only committed to the promotion of business and to the support of businesspeople rather than the administration of justice and protection of peasants, which are the duty of every ruler. They have even subjected war and peace to [the dictates of] business such that they will go to war when war is needed and will stay calm when one must stay calm. On the pretext of commercial interest they charge towards peaceful countries, not refraining from massacre and destruction. When was commerce ever [conducted] this way in previous centuries? When has governance ever meant advocacy for business and support for businesspeople? When has the administration of justice and protection of citizens ever been debased as it is [today]? When has the world ever been so chaotic and ignoble?

As they have said: the masses are the herd and the monarch or government is the shepherd. The shepherd must heed the injured and weak cattle more than the others. Do the governments in Europe heed the desolate? If they do, what remedy have they devised for the disaster of unemployment which has spread all over Europe and ruined millions of families?

These [Europeans] argue: unemployment is the result of crisis, enumerating disparate phenomena such as the war between China and Japan, the [independence] movement in India,[10] customs restrictions, fear of war in the West and so on as the causes of this crisis.

It is clear from this [argument] that statesmen in the West are not genuine with the unemployed because this assertion is deception and a scheme. With this claim [the West] wants to sidetrack the unemployed, keeping them hopeful that because unemployment is the result of contemporary events, it will pass soon. They want them [the unemployed] not to consider the machine their enemy, not harbour enmity towards it, believe their problems are the result of contemporary events, and hope that it will pass soon.

[The existence of a] crisis is nothing but a product of imagination. For as long as the world has existed, it has not been free from wars, movements and such events. Thus, crisis must have always existed. Why not tell the truth: the day machines appeared, from that day it should have been known that such results will ensue. When a machine can do the work of one hundred workers, it goes without saying that ninety-nine individuals will be left unemployed, losing the means of livelihood whether there is a war in China or not.

Even if we believe that recent events have had an impact on employment, we must say that they have only deteriorated what has [already] existed. [This is] exactly like a person who is battling an acute illness but he endures it without embarking on treatment, until in this condition he catches cold, cannot endure it any longer and becomes bed-ridden. If this man considers his illness to be solely [the result of] the cold, refusing to treat anything but the cold, is this not evidence of his ignorance?!

---

[10] The struggle for Indian independence from British colonialism has a long history, from the 1850s to India's independence in 1947. Here, Kasravi is most likely referring to the most recent episode in that struggle in 1930. Known as Civil Disobedience, this specific episode involved Mohandas Gandhi (1869–1948) openly defying the British by protesting British monopoly on Indian salt through a seaward march.

At any rate, how can a dominion be so unsettled that a war in another distant region should be the cause of unemployment for millions of people?! How is it that the crisis does not strike countries where machines and factories have not spread out of proportion?!

Leaving behind all these [arguments], what is the remedy for those helpless [people] now?! Must they not have sustenance before the crisis has been lifted from the world?!

Chapter Six

Madness

Any ailment must be cured at its root where it came from. Likewise, unemployment in Europe which is the result of machines, its remedy is nothing but eliminating machines or containing their excess. If some tasks cannot be done except with a machine, there are a host of other tasks that can be performed both manually or with machines. These tasks must not be done except manually in order to find work for the unemployed.

However, the capitalists in Europe and their governments refuse to wash their hands off machines. They have profited from machines and treasure it, even though some others have been harmed by it. To them life is a battlefield where every individual must not seek but his own self-interest. And if we hear them complain about the recent downturn in the world, it is not out of concern for the unemployed but for the lack of extravagant profits for themselves.

They say: to date more than 25,000 different proposals for solutions to the crisis have reached the Geneva association. One ailment and 25,000 remedies, and yet there is no hope for recovery. Where a genuine solution to a problem is not sought, a bogus raison d'être leads everyone to propose a different solution.

This is similar to a cholera-infested city in which the epidemic annihilates hundreds of individuals. Of necessity, the disease must be eliminated. But if a certain group of individuals does not like this solution or see in it a profit for themselves, [this leads to] resorting to a bogus remedy for which everyone will have a different proposal, and from all these proposals there will never follow a beneficial solution.

If the Europeans do not contain the ever-increasing proliferation of machines, many other adverse ordeals will follow. And with the insincerity and ignorance evident in their actions, the world will inevitably have a dreadful future.

The government of America has this to say about the unemployed in that country: 'we will restore trade to its 1929 status in which case we will not have more than five million unemployed'.[11] This is one of the proposed remedies. And since America is the leader of the capitalist world, it is safe to assert that this proposal is endorsed by all capitalists. But can America indeed restore trade to the same conditions as four years ago?! Assume that they could, what will they do with the daily proliferation of machines which will in turn reduce the need for workers in factories?! Besides, is five million unemployed (which, counting their wives and children, will not be less than twenty million) a small number?! Suppose that the day will come when you find work for all of them, how will you resolve the hardships of working-class life where their daily wages do not warrant subsistence and they are utterly deprived of repose and satisfaction?! Is the disruption of balance which is the inevitable consequence of machines resolvable?! Is the state of scores of women and young girls who toil to death in factories and mines in exchange for a small wage not a disgrace to the world?! What is the value of this hellish tool when the world is suffering from it so much?!

If machines are intended for the welfare of humans, they must be admitted insofar as they provide welfare; beyond that, [you should] throw [them] away instead of bringing so many hardships upon yourselves.

Disregarding all its other damages, it is harmful enough that machines have bewildered the world in this way; worse, it must be said that they have driven the world to madness.

What madness [is] worse than the fact that the meaning of trade and commerce has been corrupted, turning them into disasters for the world? Certain Americans who consider themselves pioneers have risen and instruct that whatever factories manufacture or weave, they must do so such that the manufactured or woven goods stop working or are torn within a short time.[12] And the reason they cite for this false claim is that in this way there will always be buyers and the machines will not be idle. It is curious that they

---

[11] It is not clear whether this is a verbatim quote or whether Kasravi is paraphrasing (as he often does) such a claim made by an American politician during the Great Depression. What is clear, however, is that Kasravi's citation refers to a series of economic reforms and relief programmes that were part of President Roosevelt's 'New Deal', a promise to Americans that these measures would contain and reverse the economic devastation brought about by the Great Depression.

[12] On the idea of planned obsolescence being evoked here, see the first note in Book 1: 8.

consider this treacherous and irrational false claim of theirs to be [a form of] advice or guidance, announcing it with their heads held high. It is even more curious that the Easterners take those false claims and publish them in their newspapers and books without being aware of the damages.

No one seems to ask these fools, twenty years ago when fabrics lasted several years, were opportunities for trade unavailable?! Is this widespread unemployment the result of fabrics and other goods lasting years that you seek such a solution [to unemployment]? How is it that your imagination extends this far but you refuse to entertain any thought of containing the spread of machines which is the real cure for this ailment?! Will this solution which you have devised bear fruit? Today you weave fabrics that won't last more than a month. Next year when there are even more machines you will weave one-week fabrics. The year beyond that one-day fabrics. Fie on such folly, fie!

The machine must work for humans and not humans for the machine. It is the result of your madness that humans waste their lives away on the path of machinism. And you are still not satisfied with this. You want them [the people] to be trapped further such that they are never relieved from want of shoes and socks and clothes.

In the same way as Machiavelli's perverse formulae have entered the field of politics,[13] what if your ill-fated false claims extend from factories to other occupations and professions? [If] physicians were to ensure the abundance of patients, or [if] builders were to erect buildings so that they crack or collapse in a short time, thereby boosting the market for their professions, what will be the state of the world with such treacherous acts?!*

On the one hand, your justification for machines is that they reduce human toil; on the other hand, the machine adds to human suffering one-hundred fold. Are you not mad?!

If nothing else, reflect upon the consequences of your actions. With all the damages you inflict upon the world and the falsehoods that you traitorously

---

[13] Kasravi's reference is to the sixteenth-century political treatise, *The Prince* (*Il Principe*), by the Italian diplomat Niccolò Machiavelli in which he argued that the same standards of virtue may not necessarily be applicable to princes, or rulers, who may be justified to use immoral or unethical means to achieve political ends.

* This dreadful scenario has found its place [in Iran]. In recent years tradesmen in Iran and some physicians have embarked on such misdeeds. There is no solution except for everyone else to devote themselves to even more good deeds so that they can undo this scheme and compel such people to abandon [such] dishonesty.

spread, will you achieve any useful result?! Today your chaotic state is so miserable that, according to your own claims, millions of your people are utterly ruined and hundreds of merchants go out [of business] because of a war between China and Japan or a movement in India. And because you do not learn a lesson, you intensify your chaotic state, what will your condition be tomorrow?!

For the world sincerity is more essential than all else. You do not possess that [sincerity] nor want to possess it; [thus] the more you exert efforts, the more harm you will add to existing ones and the end of you will be none other than destruction.

Chapter Seven

Bolshevism

On the question of machines, we must also make mention of Bolshevism. If we assess the state of the machine today, its harms and the Europeans' affection for it, it must be said that [it is similar to the story of] some persons who have embraced venomous serpents, not being concerned with their fangs while at the same time each thinking of an antidote. Alas, no antidote is beneficial.

One such antidote is Bolshevism or Mazdakism[14]: equality for all, elimination of poverty and wealth, termination of competition for survival – these are statements that appeal to everyone. But is such aspiration feasible? Today millions of people in Russia subscribe to this ideology, experimenting with it for over a decade. Even so, we do not believe that such an ideology will accomplish much in the world.

We first ask, is it plausible for food, clothes and other things to be rationed equally among humans?! Is everything suited to being rationed?! Are all humans alike so that they receive equal ration out of life's pleasures?!

If indeed things can be distributed among everyone, it is inevitable that a quarter of the population must be tasked with this activity and this in itself has many disadvantages.

The point must be made here that the lordship or dominion of one human group over another is analogous to poison used as medicine. On the one hand, we are in dire need of it but, on the other hand, we must be very vigilant to administer the correct dosage.

---

[14] Named after its Persian proponent (and possible founder) Mazdak, Mazdakism was an offshoot of Zoroastrianism in Pre-Islamic Persia. It drew on Zoroastrian dualism (the world as a stage for the confrontation between the co-eternal forces of good and evil, or light and darkness) but deviated from orthodox Zoroastrian doctrine by arguing that humanity can defeat darkness and bring light to the world through a series of ascetic practices, one of which involved abolishing private property. To the contemporary establishment, Mazdakism was a heretical movement in Sasanian Persia (224–651 CE). Kasravi deploys Mazdakism here as a proto-socialist movement in ancient Persia.

The [practice of] dominion leads most people to oppressing others. Few in a dominant position do not take pleasure in oppressing the subordinates or holding the same view of them all. This is why we should impose restrictions on the sphere of sovereignty, leaving people to be free and in peace. Those we appoint for the administration of order and security, if they are few [in terms of the numbers needed], we can find honest and fit individuals to fill the needed spaces. But if we are in need of a large group, we may not be able to find as many honest individuals.

One of the problems with Europeans is that governments constantly legislate laws and establish bureaus for anything they do, thereby limiting the people's freedom. [This is true] especially in the Bolshevik system where, as we have said, volition is extremely restricted and people will not even have the choice of food and clothing in their own hands.

If [equal] distribution of food and clothing and other necessities of life among people appears to be simple in theory, it is abundantly difficult [in practice]. The injustices that result and the suffering that ensues will be very considerable. Countless other injustices and resentments will follow as a result of uniformity of labour, adding difficulty to [the already] difficult [situation].

Where the light of life brings hope, in this system the window of hope will be closed to all. And when wise and intelligent individuals are deemed to be the same as others, inevitably talents will not be engaged and will gradually abate.

It is out of the Europeans' arrogance that they have no regard for the tried and peaceful way of life which was before humans for centuries and [instead] go astray. Do they think those who build railways also know life's ways better? But the testimony to their inexperience is that they have impudently risen to battle God and religion. It won't be long before the poisonous fruits of irreligiosity ripen and then they shall know how astray they have trodden.

As we have said, each individual must benefit from the joys of life in accordance with his God-given talents and in accordance with the efforts he has made for others' benefit. And everyone must be free in this regard. What is important, however, is that we must obstruct the illicit means and practices that are solely dedicated to amassing wealth. What governments need to do is this.

Just as highway banditry, robbery, gambling, fraud and such actions are illegal [ways of earning money] and are prevented, machine ownership is also a quick and outright way dedicated to amassing wealth and must [therefore] be prevented.

In other words, if life is a battle, all humans should have one type of apparatus to deal with each other, but not [a situation in which] one side possesses cannons with immense firepower while the other side does not have access to anything but sticks. If from the outset of the emergence of machines the foresight had been put in place so that the greedy do not use it for amassing wealth, then these problems would not appear.

At any rate, it is singularly wrong for some to propose Bolshevism as the solution to the harms of machinism and disrupt the foundation of life. However much I think, I do not see how this apparatus can have such worth that as a result of it the world must bear so many hardships and some people abandon the tried and peaceful ways of life and instead choose such a dreadful path.

This is [similar to] the story of that fool who had sat on the horse backwards. When they pointed that out to him, he said, 'I have not sat backwards; the horse is standing backwards'. Similarly, these [Europeans] have invented an apparatus that is not in accord with the world's order but instead of abandoning it, they reverse the millennial world order.

If we need another [allegorical] example to demonstrate this point, it must be said: An individual has planted a tree that bears pungent fruits. Instead of uprooting the tree, he conditions his own children to accept and eat pungent fruits.

If the machine yielded immense benefits, it would not be improper for the world to tolerate hardships or for there to be changes in people's lives. Alas, there is not much benefit in it and all this fuss over it is altogether deception as we have said elsewhere.*

What is worse is that the Russians have turned their attention towards the heavens without first settling their earthly affairs, experimenting with Bolshevism and atheism in one go.[15] It is evident from here that this is the

---

* Chapter 3 in Book I.
[15] Kasravi alludes here to the restraint placed on religious practice in communist Russia. While the Soviet state never officially outlawed religious belief, it did pursue an unofficial policy of state atheism.

work of fancy while wisdom and reflection are set aside. Suppose that some people are not devoted to religion nor benefit from its prospect, why [should the Bolshevists] blow the trumpet of atheism?! What auspicious end can one hope to attain from enmity with God?!

One of the curious inclinations of Europe is a concept they themselves call 'antithesis' and consider it a [propelling] factor of life. This means whatever is in currency today, tomorrow they will take the antithetical view. Or if some people have an idea, others accept the exact opposite.[16]

Just as in poor climes the weather is sometimes bitterly cold and sometimes unbearably hot, or [just as] certain unworthy fools vainly praise someone today while reproaching him the next, the Westerners, too, sometimes adhere to this extreme and sometimes to that in affairs and in perceptions. They seldom maintain a balance or accept the middle ground.

There is ample evidence for this claim: from that fundamentalist adherence to religion in previous centuries and the [resulting] military expeditions into the East in the name of religion and such actions that have been recorded in histories,[17] to the contemporary [approach] in which Darwinism and other [such] poisonous philosophies are adhered to.

On the one hand, there are those who believe humans to be nothing but a physical body, adamantly denying [the existence of] the soul. Vis-à-vis this crowd, a sizeable group evokes the souls of the dead, assigns numbers and levels to them, conjures them to their tables and converses with them. In their estimation, souls also can be each other's friends or enemies, kill each other, engage in lying and deception, tell jokes, play musical instruments, sing and a host of other things.

In France prior to the revolution of 1789, the accused was decapitated without trial. Today, the person who has assassinated the president in broad daylight among thousands [of witnesses], who has been caught holding a pistol and not pleaded innocence, is given hearings for weeks.

Just like impulsive youth and women who follow a different fashion every day and every time adopt new manners, the Westerners, too, consider life's

---

[16] Kasravi's term in Persian is 'bargasht' which carries the literal sense of reverse or return. It has been translated as 'antithesis' because it is highly likely that here Kasravi - in his usual allusive style and given his arguments in the rest of the chapter - is critiquing Hegel's dialectic theory of historical and philosophical progress, which comprises of thesis, antithesis and synthesis.
[17] Kasravi's reference is to the Crusades.

most important affairs in the same way, and in the name of 'antithesis' everyday they undertake to do the opposite of the previous day. What is more curious is that they reproach Easterners who are not impulsive and ignorant as them, calling them [the Easterners] 'lifeless' and 'frozen!'

Just as Russia's Bolshevism is the antithesis of Western Europe's capitalism, their irreligiosity is the antithesis of the religious fundamentalism which existed in that country before the Bolshevik revolt. Just as that [condition] has no cause but misguidance and ignorance, this [state], too, is based upon audacity and impudence. If perceptiveness and reason are the criteria, how has that religious fundamentalism turned into this audacious irreligiosity?! Has anyone returned from the invisible world, bringing news [of the other world] from behind the curtain screening the unseen?[18] Or what irrefutable evidence has been obtained to warrant their flying the banner of atheism in this manner?!

They underestimate [the consequences of] irreligiosity and do not yet know what calamity they face. But soon the bitter and heart-rending fruits of this inauspicious tree will ripen, and it will be known that day what false path they have trodden.

---

[18] In Islamic thought, metaphysical truths are said to be behind a metaphorical curtain or veil. Quran 50:22, for example.

Chapter Eight

Three pillars of life

We won't admonish the West any longer. The basis of our argument is that if Europe has invented wondrous instruments or made some progress in certain sciences, the result of these wonders and advancements is not peace and happiness but a series of problems.

The West's achievements and wonders are not attended by [a corresponding] consciousness or awareness of the world's benefit or harm. Rather, as we have said, the Westerners are quite bankrupt in this regard, devoid of consciousness and awareness.

Advocates of Europe disproportionately glorify Europeans' [invention of] aero planes, automobiles, railroads, the electrical lamp, telegraph, telephone, cinema, radio and other [such] inventions and whenever there is talk of Europe, they uphold these wondrous achievements with much clamour. However, as we have said, the result of these inventions does not go beyond the fact that these inventions have changed the instruments of life [by replacing old ones]. However, these inventions do not have much impact on human life and the benefits enumerated for them are mostly deception and lies.

Human life is erected upon three pillars: first, ethos of coexistence; second, laws; third, disposition. If we need further clarification, it must be said that when a community have gathered in a place, they need to coexist. What makes this coexistence auspicious or inauspicious is three things: first, how members of the community treat each other: do they aid each other joining hands like brothers or do they confront each other like enemies? And this is what we mean by ethos of coexistence. Second, what is the nature of their rule [over each other], supported by which laws or administrative apparatus? Third, what disposition does each member [of the community] have?

We have asserted [this] in the appropriate place [above]: the problems of humans and what entangles them in suffering and torment is the catastrophic competition they have with each other in the battlefield of life. However, the more moderate this competition is within a community, the more happiness and repose there will be [among them].

We now declare: the severity or moderation of this human competition is dependent upon how well or how poorly those three pillars of life are [implemented]. If a community's principles of coexistence and their laws are sensible and [if they] have commendable dispositions, then conflict and competition among them will abate even as tranquillity and happiness increase. Otherwise, the conflict will escalate, not leaving room for welfare and happiness.

At any rate, Europe's inventions are not compliant with these observations and weigh light on the [proverbial] scale of the world's benefit and harm. This is because these inventions do not amount to more than this: individuals riding an automobile or airplane instead of a horse; or some people lighting their rooms with electricity rather than with tallow or olive seed oil; or weaving clothes and socks with machines rather than by hand. Are these things that play a role in creating communal happiness and welfare?! Granted, if machines did not have the harms we have enumerated, it would reduce human toil. Alas, their harms are so numerous that they obscure the benefits.

We address the Easterners: give Europe's inventions and scientific discoveries their due value but abstain from falsity and exaggeration. Likewise, distinguish between the beneficial and the harmful in adopting them. Military technologies, armaments and whatever is the cause of states' empowerment must all be obtained [from Europe]. Telegraph, telephones, automobiles, electricity, airplanes, extensive networks of railroads, because these are the cause of states' power, nothing can be said about them [i.e. they are necessary]. Professional machinery, which is gradually taking hold, must be obtained where manual production does not suffice. But where there is no need for them, beware that you do not obtain [them] and avoid entrapping yourselves in their harms.

Worthy sciences such as medicine, astronomy and the like must be learned. Who is to say that the East will not be the home of these sciences in future?

In any case, what befits discussion is these inventions and sciences, but we must never take the discussion in other directions. In other words, if Europe has been triumphant, has progressed, and has found ascendancy over others, it is only limited to the field of discovery and invention and nothing else. In other respects, the situation is entirely reversed, especially regarding those three important pillars of life in respect to which we must be resolutely weary of and keep our distance from Europe. It is easily viable to learn Europe's inventions and sciences while avoiding its other offerings. If certain people learn [from] Europe's artistry its positive achievements, why will it be difficult to hold back from its [Europe's] reprehensible qualities and ways of life?! Especially if these same people have superior qualities and far better ways of life.

One point must always be kept in mind: Easterners are far superior to Westerners in regard to the principles of coexistence and ethos of humanity.

We repeat that the industries and sciences of Europe must be distinguished from its ethos of coexistence and laws and dispositions; from the perspective of Easternism, we must erect a wall between the two.[19]

Some find it difficult to believe that Europeans, after having amassed so much knowledge and achieved so many wondrous feats, cannot distinguish between the world's benefit and harm. This misconception has afflicted the Westerners themselves more than others, [assuming] that because they have attained inventions they have also changed the rules of life. It must be known that manufacturing machines and other such achievements are not the same thing as distinguishing between the world's benefit and harm. Even if in previous centuries certain wise men arose from Europe, establishing some wise principles, today there is a very slight trace of those principles left as a result of the emergence of false indoctrinations, hegemony of the greedy, and spread of coercion and deception. Whether we like it or not, today Europe has the basest existence and has gravitated towards degradation in every respect. If a tree must be known by its fruit, Europe's current condition is the best testimony that their way of life is the most irrational way, and this claim is never deniable.

---

[19] Easternism is the literal equivalent to Kasravi's coinage *sharqi-gari* It has been translated as 'Easternism' for consistency with his other coinage, *urupā'i-gari* or 'Europism'. He contrasts the two, citing 'Easternism' as the appropriate alternative for the people of the East. His specific proposal here is that we must learn and benefit from Europe's scientific and technological advances, but we must not follow their mannerisms, laws or dispositions.

Chapter Nine

Misguided guides

If we assess the current condition of Eastern countries such as Egypt, Ottoman [Turkey], Syria, Iran, Iraq, Afghanistan and India in relation to Europe, it is akin to a group [of individuals] who have gathered in a house, not having any idea or answers about life; therefore they direct their eyes towards the neighbour's house, following whatever they see or hear there and never concerning themselves with right and wrong or benefit and harm.

Presently, all these regions, whether distant from or close to each other, are treading the path of Europism, considering it the path to progress and ascendency and calling other countries to join in.

Whence has this situation arisen?! Have some wise individuals deliberated together and chosen this path?!

Alas not! In the previous centuries the East was not turbulent or chaotic enough to warrant it to reflect upon its affairs or to have its wise men deliberate upon the right path. In fact, it has been the turbulence and chaos [resulting from Europe's dominance over world affairs] that has opened this path [of Europism] to the Easterners.

We know the fate of these lands over the past centuries: nomadic tribes rise from the far east and charge towards these lands.[20] These incursions which lasted several consecutive centuries not only bring about the destruction of cities and towns but they also inflict other severe damages. Law and custom depart and the control of affairs falls into the hands of oppression and power. Monarchy, which had meant protection of people, loses its meaning and becomes the plaything of [individuals'] whims. Dynasties come and go one after the other. Neighbouring states do not spare each other pillage, armed incursions and bloodshed.

[20] Here Kasravi discusses what he perceived to be the immediate and longterm consequences of the thirteenth century Mongol invasion of West and Central Asia.

Religion, which is the foundation of our existence, is divided into hundreds of sects, becoming another pretext for resentment and bloodshed.

With helpless and weakened states as well as scattered and ignorant populations, everything loses its splendour and no man capable of leadership is found in the East. In this condition we encounter Europe, a Europe powerful and capable, orderly and majestic, supported by a series of inventions and skills and enjoying universal fame and name. This is where the aberration occurs and everyone thinks that we must pursue Europe, no one knowing the harms in this pursuit.

Especially since at that time Europe was in a different state in which the bitter fruits of machines had not ripened and the philosophers' scepticism had not done its damage. Europeans spoke of liberty and fraternity and there was no sign of the present injustices.

This is why the path of Europism was opened before the people. The laws of Europe spread everywhere. European practices were circulated among men and women. Gradually some individuals appeared who admired whatever belongs to Europe and despised whatever belongs to the East. And, as we pointed out, today a sizeable part of the East wishes for nothing except following the West.

This [state of] servility is not befitting the East. Even if this state were exhibited by the blacks of Africa, it would be disgraceful, let alone the people of Asia, let alone those from among whom great prophets and philosophers arose and revealed the path of salvation to the world!

Imagine a certain family possesses their own water well which has crumbled and is in a ruined state; is it their obligation to reclaim and mend the well and benefit from its delectable water, or [does it make sense] to neglect it and bring pungent and unpleasant water from the neighbours' houses for consumption?!

It is not an exaggeration that the way of life revealed by the prophets is the supreme path and if some seek the world's welfare and happiness, they must tread that path. Ours is a measured and tried assertion [on account of the historical East's lived experience], and others will make no other assertion except this if they, too, measure and try [the same experience].

If the state of the East has been chaotic, we must endeavour to find a remedy, even if this remedy means adopting some European laws. Witness to the fact that the East's disarray can be remedied is that in recent years as a result of Europe's pressure, or thanks to the encounter with it, a series of those disorders have disappeared. Presently Easterners everywhere have awakened and know what is to be done. Everywhere powerful states have emerged and the people have learned to make common cause with their governments and support their power and interests. As well, those foolish practices [committed] in the name of religion have become less frequent everywhere.

It is a misfortune that most Easterners, especially those who have hoisted the banner of Europism, do not know the East. Many of them not only do not know the meaning of prophethood and do not comprehend the benefit and value of the prophets' ordinances, but they also are uninformed about the history of the East and its golden eras.

As soon as they read criticisms of prophets in Europeans' books, they renounce them [the prophets] and take to irreligiosity, without themselves making inquiries in order to understand or use their own judgment to evaluate the prophets' prescriptions. It is sufficient testimony to their ignorance that they choose the false teachings of Western philosophers which mostly resemble delirium over the worthy ordinances of the messengers of God. Humanism which is the foundation of religion has become despised among them, while they respect Darwinism which is the order of the beasts' existence. Similar to an infant that is amused by the lines and spots on a snake, stretching its hand towards it without concern for its fatal venom, these people are also mesmerized by the Wests' wondrous feats and have taken the path of Europism without avoiding its harms.

Indeed, they do not understand that manufacturing machines and understanding the world's benefit or harm are different things. And if some people show mastery in technology and industry, this is not a reason for their superior ways of life. Even though Europe's woes are increasing daily and we witness it with our eyes, these people foolishly and brazenly every day bring new annunciations of the West's progress and supremacy and naively embrace the Westerners' futile solutions to unemployment and war and other problems, fastening their hopes to them.

A group of wayfarers who move behind each other, if a sinkhole or bog appears before them and the leader falls or sinks in it, of necessity the others reverse their direction and the leader will also return and save himself. But these Easterners who are following the West and encourage the populace to do the same, even though they see that their leader is in deep trouble without any hope of deliverance, even so they do not change their direction. They are so captivated and infatuated [with the West] that they never imagine Europe to be helpless and have high hopes that it will soon be delivered from its troubles.

They have eyes but they do not see; they have ears but they do not hear; they have hearts but they do not perceive.[21] Pity, oh pity! Woe to those who have these [Europeans] as their leaders.

---

[21] Kasravi's Persian paraphrase from Quran 7:179: 'And certainly We have created for hell many of the Jinn and the men; they have hearts with which they do not understand, and they have eyes with which they do not see, and they have ears with which they do not hear; they are as cattle, nay, they are in worse errors; these are the heedless ones'.

Chapter Ten

The ethos of coexistence

We now elaborate on each of the three important pillars of life: the ethos of coexistence, laws and dispositions:

Human life is different from animals' [life] in two ways:

First, humans possess reason which they abide by in life.

The other is that humans live in cooperative communities so every individual must not only pursue his own interests but also pursue the interests of the community as well.

In other words, when a community has gathered in one place, each member must abstain from harassing and harming others and from deception and lies and [he must] not withhold his aid and good will as much as he can from the other members, desiring communal welfare and being aware that his own well-being is connected with others' well-being.

This type of coexistence is what some ancients called 'civility' since cities and towns have appeared due to this type of coexistence.* Iranians, too, called this [type of coexistence] 'humanistic' because it does not befit humans to live life except in this manner.

A perfect example of this humanistic coexistence is clans. In each clan the elderly, the young, the powerful and the weak live equally, refraining staunchly from harassing or harming each other and from lies and deception. When one of them is destitute or ill, others communally sympathize with him and each individual seeks his satisfaction in nothing except the satisfaction of others. Every individual is always concerned that if he admits loss or harm to others, or if he lies, others will also do the same, and in this way the order of the clan will be disrupted and enmity will replace fraternity and kinship.

---

* [See] Book I, Chapter 12.

From the perspective of reason, the whole world is nothing but a clan and an upright man is he who treats the whole world as brothers. If some cannot do this, at least they must consider the region or city in which they live as a clan, walking with everyone [there] as brothers. Laws must also be founded upon such a principle.

We are not claiming that life does not need competition. There must be competition among humans, but not in a bestial way. Everyone must benefit from life in accordance with his capability and with the amount of effort he exerts towards communal benefit. Competition must be limited to this, not everyone robbing others of their belongings unjustly or with coercion, deception and lies. Laws must set limits for individuals so that they cannot cross that line.

This is what we call the principles of coexistence; this is the foundation of every community's well-being; this is the greatest and worthiest thing in the world; this is what God's elect have sought for the world, enduring all that hardship on this path. It has been thanks to their efforts that this principle has taken hold more or less in the world and was common practice everywhere for centuries. As testimony, remnants of it are still evident in the East. In the West before this movement [i.e. machinism], it was also common for a few centuries.

Indeed, in the East it did not suffice to give kindness or aid to other humans; some people attempted [to instruct] that each individual always choose others' well-being over his own and seek people's benefit even at the expense of loss to himself. As a justification [for this claim], the foundation of Sufism, which was widespread in Iran and surrounding regions for centuries, was [informed by] this same instruction.

Now let us see what is happening in the West and what principles the Europeans propose for existence. If a tree must be known by its fruit, it must be said that Europe has the worst principles for existence because we all know that in that land of electricity and steam [engines], the worst conditions have emerged.

As we have said, hostile grudges, destabilization of the foundation of religion, false teachings of irreligious philosophers, emergence of machines, spread of greed, division [of society] into the affluent and the poor: these are the things that have entangled Europe and penetrated the foundations of humanism.

In a place where the affluent and the poor seek to shed each other's blood and [where] the powerful deem the powerless to be deserving of annihilation, in such a place what cannot be found is kindness and collaboration.

In a place where some in the name of [being] learned or philosophers rise and dishearten people in regard to humanity, calling them to follow beasts, in such a place humanism cannot be sought.

It would have been better if these philosophers lived in deserts and mountains teaching philosophy to lions and leopards and wolves. Otherwise how is it just to indoctrinate humans with such prescriptions?!

It must be said bluntly: Europe has lost the ethos of humanity and its contemporary state is the worst state that has been witnessed from the outset of history to the present. Likewise, any country that follows it will inevitably be in a similar state. Alas, there is no remedy for these ailments and once a population is entangled [in these problems] it will meet no end but destruction.

This is where wise men deprecate Europe and address it in this manner: you can do anything except living as humans because the manner of living Europe has chosen befits beasts, not humans.

It is not befitting the noblest among God's creations that one group master over others, monopolize all of life's pleasures, deprive the weak of everything and not sympathize with their wretched state.

If we put together all of Europe's inventions and discoveries, from automobiles and the railroad to the numerous [chemical] elements that they have discovered or the microbes they have uncovered, they have as much value as a blade of straw when compared with the ethos of humanity. It behooves humans to adhere to humanity and if a people do not do so, they have incurred loss, even if they have hundreds of achievements.

The ethos of humanity for the world is tantamount to health for a human being. However, Europe's inventions and sciences, even if we were to judge them all as beneficial, are tantamount to the goldsmiths' technique by which they craft wondrous golden or silver tools. Likewise, the state of Europe is akin to a person who does not look after his own health, ignoring it utterly, while his only amusement is that he has learned the goldsmith's art well and has made countless golden and silver tools for himself. Does not such a man incur loss?!

Flying to the sky, conversing from a distance of hundreds of miles, treading hundreds of miles of road in one hour, dispatching messages using electricity, and other such wondrous activities: how have these benefited Europe when tranquillity and contentment have departed from scores of its homes, [when] one-third of its population is either hungry and exposed or pass their days in the harshest of conditions?!

What benefit do all these electrical lamps lighting the streets and houses have for those who sleep hungry at nights under their light?! Those millions of unemployed [persons] who find the doors to sustenance closed to them, or those scores of workers who barely earn plain bread for their daily toil, what joy lights up their hearts on account of airplanes flying over their heads or radios bringing sounds from distant places to their ears?!

Considering the way in which Europeans pursue trade, the recklessness with which amassing wealth has become the order of the day, the affection that has been attached to machinery, we preach about humanism in vain! It might as well be said that the Europeans do not seek such ideals and [instead] elevate machinism and profiteering, as they practice it, over all else!

Among Europe's undertakings which deserve applause are their good deeds in previous centuries [such as] abolishing feudalism and instituting the principles of liberty and equality and other such good deeds which have been described in histories. Alas, there is little sign of those good deeds today. Today the state of Europe is worse than the feudal era.

It is enough testimony to Europe's grave condition today that Bolshevism emerged from there. This is because the masses are exposed to such excessive pressures and scarcity that they scramble in every direction, submitting themselves to every manner of hardship and struggle.

If instead of all these inventions and discoveries a man of God rose from Europe and revived the ethos of humanity there, liberating the people from entrapment, such a person would be Europe's 'saviour' and would have primacy over all the artists and philosophers and inventors.

Chapter Eleven

Brotherly treatment

Certain individuals are so taken with Europe's grandeur and external splendour that they are truly dazzled and do not recognize but instead resist our assertions as much as they can. In regard to these [arguments above] they will perhaps insist that that type of existence to which you refer is unthinkable. In their estimation the world today is as it has [always] been and will [always] be. On the contrary many of them show utmost ignorance in asserting that the more the world marches towards progress, the more increased life's hardships will be.

We call upon these persons to study history to find out what state of tranquillity the world had been in some seven or eight centuries ago, especially in the East where the ethos of humanity prevailed far and wide.

We have said many times and will assert it again: on the path of Europism not only does the world not progress and find ascendancy, it will devolve into degradation. The claim that life's hardship will increase [with progress] is itself testimony to the world's degradation. Misguided are those who consider this a sign of progress! If it is true that the world seeks convenience and contentment (as Europe also makes this claim), then it goes without saying that the daily increase in toil and hardship in the world is justification for the world's devolution and disconnect from its goal.

Historians living seven or eight centuries ago have written accounts of the people's tranquillity in those times and of the acts of kindness they showed each other which seem highly extraordinary at this time. Advocates of Europe should read those accounts to better understand the meaning of the world's superiority and ascendancy.

Estakhri, who was a fourth-century explorer, writes an account of the hospitality of the inhabitants of Sogdia which is astounding.[22] He writes,

> 'In much of this land [it is] as if all the inhabitants lived in the same house. When someone visits a house, it is as if he arrived at his own dwelling since not only does the host not feel bothered by the visitor but endeavours as much as he can to entertain and indulge him, even if the visitor is a stranger. They do this not in hopes of reward but due to [their] generosity. Every person has no wish except to offer hospitality within his means'.

He writes,

> 'I saw the entrance to a residence nailed to the wall so that it is never closed [to visitors] and I heard that it has not been closed in one hundred years and will remain open to posterity. Often at night one or two hundred or more persons arrive there unexpectedly and alight accompanied with their cattle. For all of them edibles and accommodation and for their cattle hay and barely is on hand without any hardship or trouble for the host because this is his usual practice.
>
> Most Sogdians expend whatever they earn toward building monasteries, mending roads, and jihad[23] and other such good deeds, except a few among them who are bereft of such generosity. You will not find any city or pond or a wilderness en route [to another place] or a hamlet or village without public inns having been erected there, more than what is required for wayfarers'.

He further writes: 'I have heard that in all of Sogdia there are in excess of ten thousand public inns, in most of which provisions are provided [for free] for a traveller and his steed from the time he arrives until the time he leaves'.

Muhammad the son of Battuta [Ibn Battuta] was an inhabitant of Tangier and an eighth-century explorer.[24] He travelled for twenty years in the Hejaz,

---

[22] Kasravi's reference is to Abu Ishāq Ibrahim ibn-Muhammad al-Farsi, known as Estakhri (d. 957 CE). Kasravi's dating is in reference to the Hijri calendar. Sogdia (also Sogdiana) was an ancient Iranian civilization, its heartland based, roughly, in the provinces of Samarkand and Bukhara as well as Sughd in modern-day Uzbekistan and Tajikistan, respectively.

[23] In its classical use, jihad literally means effort or struggle. It refers to any endeavour for the protection or betterment of self and the community. It is being used in this sense here.

[24] Ibn Battuta (1304–1368/9), a Moroccan geographer, scholar and explorer (sometimes referred to as the 'Muslim Marco Polo'), travelled much of the lands of Islam (or Dar al-Islam) from the Middle East, Central Asia and Eurasia to south and southeast Asia and China over a period of thirty years. The expanse of lands he travelled exceeds that of Marco Polo almost fivefold. The account of his journeys was collected in a volume commonly known as the *Rihla*. Kasravi's dating is in reference to the Islamic Hijri calendar.

Syria, Iraq, Iran, the Kipchak Plains,[25] Ottoman lands, the northern parts of the Caspian Sea, Turkistan, India, China and the Sudan, also travelling to Istanbul which was still under Roman rule. His *Rihla* (Travels) is an exceedingly engaging read. Even though at that time Iran and those regions had seen much damage from the Mongol [invasions], losing much of their splendour and bustle, even so the stories this man relates – from the people's kindness to each other to generosity, charity, support for the poor and hospitality – are truly awe-inspiring. At that time Sufism was at its peak and instead of Europe's factionalism today, there was in Ottoman lands and those regions a society known as Knightly Men,[26] one of whose activities was looking after wayfarers and strangers.

This was done in this manner: in every city a group of young people, especially those who had not taken a wife, would choose one among themselves [as a leader] and would gather around him. Each of them would give him what they had earned from their daily trade. Then at nights they would gather at the monastery and after prayers and mentioning [the name of] God, they would engage in merriment and festivity and consumed all manners of edibles. They would also task some among them to keep watch for strangers who arrived from a journey, especially Sufis, and to then lead them to the monastery. They would merrily welcome whoever arrived there and set out to entertain them. First they would send [the guest] to the bathhouse, giving him new clothes. For as long as he stayed, they would not withhold any manner of kindness or indulgence and when he intended to depart, they would give him clothes, money and whatever he needed.

The son of Battuta writes: "In some towns there were two groups of the Knightly Men who would quarrel with each other over who should host us. We had to spend a few days with one group and then go to the other group."

In those days in Iran and other regions they would build monasteries in villages that were located en route [to major towns] for hosting wayfarers,

---

[25] Kipchak plains refer to an expansive territory in the Eurasian steppe (from the Aral Sea in the east to the Black Sea in the west) peopled by a loose confederation of nomadic Turkish tribes in the Medieval Period (roughly, the tenth to the thirteenth centuries). Islam became the majority religion among Kipchaks following the Mongol conquest of Central Asia in the thirteenth century.

[26] Kasravi's term is 'javānmardān'. Literally meaning 'young men', the term has a long history and profound connotation in Persian culture. The *javānmard* embodied strength of body and character, honour, manliness and virtue. One of his main tasks was to protect not only the community's safety but also its honour. The closest equivalent to this figure in European literature would probably be the figure of the knight-errant. Also see related note on *futuwwa* in Book 1:15.

and because [the word] monastery translates into 'zāviyeh' [corner] in Arabic, most of those villages are named after it. This is why today we have many villages carrying the name 'corner' in Azerbaijan [province] and other places.[27]

In many towns in Iran selling bread was considered a dishonour and no one would sell it, just as today we do not sell water. Whoever arrived in a town or a village and was hungry, he would knock on any door and would receive bread without paying a price.

We remember that even until thirty or so years ago, before calls to Europism appeared, the affluent in Iran would hold public feasts several times a year, inviting their kin, neighbours and the poor, especially during the months of Muharram and Ramadan when public feasts were held aplenty in mosques and places of worship.

At that time the disease of greed did not exist and whoever became wealthy opened his hand in generosity and charity. This was why there were neither too many wealthy individuals nor were the poor bereft of life's enjoyments altogether, harbouring resentment against the wealthy. People lived a brotherly existence together.

---

[27] The village Zāvieh Kord in Ardabil province in northwestern Iran, for instance, would have been so named because it hosted the monastic inn that might have been built or perhaps maintained by local Kurds; thus, the village itself would have been called 'Kurdish Monastery' or Zāvieh Kord. Kasravi's point here is that the practice of hospitality and aiding strangers had been so widespread that it was reflected even in the names assigned to towns and villages.

Chapter Twelve

Agricultural works

This was the noble existence our ancestors led.

Every individual endeavoured to be remembered by his charity and open-handedness, and they competed against each other in lending a hand to the poor and the downtrodden. That, and only that, was the [meaning of] ascendancy in the world.

It is as a result of their hawkishness and bellicosity that the Europeans trumpet their superiority around the world, despite their own starve-infested society and the ruthlessness with which the affluent treat the poor and the wretched.

They only know how to constantly manufacture machines and mobilize weaponry, devil may care about [what happens to] the world. Conceited with these achievements, they sing their own praises and have filled the world with self-praise.

Today millions of people are hungry in Europe and we know many have relinquished their homes and sent their children on the streets. We hear some commit suicide out of hunger. We must find whence this penury has come about.

The advocates of Europe will each give an explanation. However, the truth is that as a result of the appearance of machines the balance of life has been disrupted. And all these [problems] are the consequence of imbalance.

The basis of existence is eating, sleeping, breathing and being healthy; afterwards there is need for clothing. This is why the best trade is agricultural works. Why? Because as a result of this trade there will be an abundance of sustenance and everyone from the poor to the affluent will benefit.

If instead of the energy spent on tool making Europe embarked on improvements in sowing and planting, it would be better and ten times more profitable; the world would be filled with blessing and poverty and starvation would disappear; instead of living in smoke-filled and polluted cities, people would live in green and lavish villages; instead of greed and amassing wealth, charity and open-handedness would become widespread. However, instead of improving agricultural works, Europe has undertaken to undermine it. Since the day factories were established, agriculture has waned.

And then Europe's machines have also resulted in people everywhere being busy with self-beautification. The constant need to refine [their] clothes, hats and shoes has made them so entangled that they are less concerned with daily bread and other necessities of life. This is specially the case in cities where women and men stomach unsavoury edibles, breathe in dust-filled and polluted air, deprived of restful sleep, unable to attend to their health, [all because] day and night they have no concern except clothes and self-beautification, spending all they earn from their professions on colourful garments and various adornments.

In this infernal existence, how can one create public houses for entertaining wayfarers? How can one embark upon aiding the downtrodden? How can one be concerned about relatives and neighbours?! Instead, some will even defraud others in order to afford the excessive cost of their foppery.

Despite its other drawbacks, this problem is also detrimental to agriculture because, on the one hand, agriculturalists have to sell their harvest at high prices due to hefty costs or sustain a loss. On the other hand, people's commitments and the burdensome costs they must shoulder is the cause of their cutting back on food, this leading to stagnation in agriculture. If today there is an excess of grain and other harvest rotting in silos, it is not because of abundance but because a majority of people cannot afford to eat to [their] satisfaction. They can hardly afford bread, potatoes and the like, let alone delightful edibles such as various sweet fruits, sugar, nectar, tea, coffee and such.

If Europe's actions were based on knowledge and wisdom, they should endeavour to improve agricultural works and make those God-given gifts abundant and cheap so that people can benefit and be healthy, thereby looking after and assisting the downtrodden on full stomachs and without greed.

Is it not foolishness that some boast about industry and sometimes refer to 'industrial self-sufficiency' while one-third of their populations is deprived of free God-given gifts, worse, a majority of them rarely experience [the joy of] a full stomach?! Is industrial self-sufficiency essential for them, but not immunity from hunger?!

The Bolsheviks have been striving for years and now according to them they have reached the level of the great powers in terms of machinery and factories. This is why they praise themselves while we know what turmoil exists among them on account of starvation.

Can one find a trace of wisdom and knowledge in these actions?! Will the end of this ignorance be anything except annihilation?! Ignoble [are] those who are envious of the abundance and tranquillity of the Easterners' life and thus lead them towards the Westerners' [wretched] condition through deception and public outcry. So much praise for Europe but no one asks so what is this hunger [which afflicts Europeans]?! If it is as a result of their superiority and progress that people are afflicted with hunger and are deprived of the world's free blessings, then let there not be such superiority!

Chapter Thirteen

The laws of Europe [introductory remarks]

The laws of Europe call for a separate book so that justice can be done to the discussion of their advantages and disadvantages. Here we can only touch upon them:

In previous centuries, there were some movements in Europe thanks to which a series of worthy and beneficial laws emerged. Europe's principles of governance are very wise. Also people's freedom and their equality before the law is highly commendable. The seeds of these ideas were planted by devout philosophers in the ancient times from which some seedlings grew, particularly in the soils of Islam where these seedlings became fruitful trees. Muslims lived for centuries by these principles until the East's condition was disrupted and power and oppression prevailed (as we have outlined above).

However, the Europeans spread liberty and equality in their region thanks to the efforts and sacrifices in recent centuries and from there [these ideals] have reached the East again. This is the only step the West has taken towards the world's progress and ascendancy. If some people boast [about Europe], they should not boast except about these contributions. We attribute these good deeds to the name of Europe and express our gratitude to noblemen who endeavoured on this path.

But it must not be concealed that these principles are one thing but Europe's current situation [is quite] another. It must be asked of the Europeans: how is your current state [to be explained] considering those movements in the previous century? When a people enshrines liberty and equality in its laws, viewing all humans as equals, how is it that in every city a group [of elites] among them has subjugated millions of families and closed the doors of sustenance upon them?!

What kind of equality is this when some are steeped in indulgence while numerous others are deprived of all enjoyment?! Or what kind of fraternity is it when one person has erected thirty-story palaces while another has relinquished his home and sent his children on the streets out of desolation?!

To the people of France who are so proud of themselves for having uprooted the feudal order, answer [this question]: were the feudal serfs more desolate or today's unemployed and hungry?! When did people die or commit suicide out of hunger under feudalism?!

Those who abolished the slave trade, thus elevating humanity's name, where are they to see people willingly setting up circumstances for their own incarceration out of need?! Which one is harder, slavery or starvation and ill-fated death?!

Alas, the world was progressing in that fashion due to some great men establishing the ethos of liberty and equality with their blood until the emergence of machines and other such nuisance hindered this progress.

In any case, Iran and other Eastern countries have done very well to adopt these values from Europe, but in doing so they have committed a grave mistake. By way of explication, there are but a few worthy among Europe's laws. The rest of its laws are utterly ill-advised. However, the Easterners consider all of Europe's laws praiseworthy, adopting and spreading each and every one of them, and this itself is a grave mistake.

Here we will not write all we know about Europism so that others do not perceive it as radicalism. But how can one react to the fact that certain groups in the East, the home of legislation, have gathered, borrowing laws from most distant lands?! What is more harmful than this?!

Law is a significant element in the life of any community but just as sensible laws are advantageous and must be cherished, ill-advised laws are disadvantageous and must be avoided. However, the advocates of Europe do not have this sense. They know nothing but propagating in the East anything that exists in Europe, whether it is good or bad.

If we did not have [our own] laws, or if Europe's laws were better, then there would be no room for criticism. But the point is that the Easterners lose the tried and measured laws they have had and instead adopt injudicious laws. This itself is inferiority, a subordination one must never submit to.

If some people do not believe that Europe's laws are harmful, we will mention some reasons for it:

We have learned from Europe to establish many schools for children and youths. This was a very beneficial undertaking and everyone, either woman or man, must be literate. But the system for this education which we have also taken from Europe is exceedingly wrong.

We have discarded elementary schools and speak of high schools: in the olden days young adults from the age of fifteen learned a trade under the tutelage of their father or another master. At the age of twenty or so, they would attain the status of manhood and could live freely and independently. This is what we have witnessed with our own eyes and remember clearly. However, today every young adult squanders six or seven years of his life in the high school and whatever he studies, either he does not understand or will soon forget. When he exits [the school] he does not stoop to any job on account of pride in the little learning he has acquired, becoming eternally vagrant and hapless. Or if he does accept a job, he needs years to learn a trade or a profession and find his way in life.

This is besides the fact that the gathering of a group of young and unseasoned persons in one place is itself cause for corruption and generates much harm, particularly in regard to girls which is utterly concerning and [they] might become ill-fated as long as they live.

If some people ask for basic literacy, this end can be achieved through elementary schools but if they seek knowledge, this end cannot be achieved through high schools. Launching into many subjects and learning a little from each is fruitless toil and a waste of one's life. As we witness, much of this education is soon forgotten. Even if it is not forgotten, it does not have equal value to six or seven precious years of life. We are also experienced and aware that this assortment of subjects erodes the youths' intelligence while diminishing their aptitude.

It must be known that not everyone is fit for higher learning. In other words, higher learning is not suitable for everyone; not everyone can benefit or profit from it.

And then unless someone pursues higher learning of their own volition, it has no result but the erosion of intelligence and potential. It would be much better if instead of these schools, they hold free evening classes. In this way: for every group of related sciences there should be a [special] school which opens in the evenings and runs lectures for two hours daily. The youth or anyone else engage in their trade during the day and go to school in the evening. After studying for one year or longer, they take exams and sign a bond that whenever there is need for their speciality in a government office or elsewhere, they will accept [the job]; otherwise they will continue to live proudly on their own trade. This and only this is the best system of education, because not only is the government relieved of costly expenses, but the youth also do not waste their life and talents at the same time becoming immune to impudence and other bad manners which are the fruits of schools. They will also not be left behind in learning a trade or profession or in the battle of life. Not only will they not have to undermine their honour at the feet of this or that person for a job, but there will also not be an excess of doctors, lawyers, engineers or such professionals who can become the cause of harassment for people and for each other (the way they are in Europe).

Some will argue that two hours daily of schooling is not sufficient for learning the subjects. We respond that if they study the subject willingly, two hours are equal to two days [of learning] that is not undertaken following one's volition. Only for medicine and the military sciences and the like might two hours not be sufficient and one must spend a whole day [on them].

In regard to girls, the harm of these schools is greater. A beautiful and precious being that has specific purposes in life and must learn whatever there is to learn by the age of fourteen or fifteen suddenly becomes involved in a series of futile subjects and talent erosion, squandering six years of her precious life, losing her God-given simplicity which is her best embellishment, becoming deprived of the very beneficial lessons which she must learn at home under the supervision of her mother – and in exchange for all these losses what advantage do they gain?!

A girl must learn lessons in hygiene and child-rearing and housewifery. What benefit is Arabic morphology and syntax, the French language, algebra, geometry or such talent-eroding subjects to her?!

Chapter Fourteen

The laws of Europe [on taxation and state administration]

Iran has been a monarchy for thousands of years [financed] through taxes on villages and farms; there have been laws for this practice which are the inevitable result of the intelligence and trials of thousands of state accountants and administrators, managing this system quite well until at the outset of the Constitutional Movement[28] this was abolished in the name of Europism. They [then] brought in some among the Europeans on hefty salaries and established law and the current modern administration. Let the advocates of Europe explain what was wrong with those ancient Iranian laws and what is advantageous about these modern laws?

From what we know those Iranian laws were very simple and easy [to implement] which, in comparison to today's laws and administration, needed one-tenth of the bureaucrats and state officials and one-hundredth of the paper usage. This is why if at that time there was need for ten accountants and officers to collect tax from a village, today there is need for one hundred. If at that time one ass-load of paper was used, today one hundred ass-loads are used. Also, if at that time an error occurred in [estimating] the tax dues of a village or an orchard, or if the process was interrupted by another task, it would be remedied in one sitting, but today it takes months to do such a task.

We have said this before and assert it again: those who possess their own fountain of wholesome water which has now crumbled and is in a ruined state, it is their obligation to reclaim and refine it and benefit from its water, not to bring pungent and unpleasant water from the neighbours' houses for their own

---

[28] Kasravi is referring to the series of public demands as well as the subsequent uprising that led to the establishment of a constitutional monarchy in Iran in 1906–7. See also related note in Book 1:10.

consumption. If that traditional system of accounting had some deficiencies, some individuals could have remedied those deficiencies, but this [situation] never merited the wholesale abolishment of that [system] and its replacement with European laws with hefty costs, especially considering the advantages of the former and the drawbacks of the latter. Even if they had to make changes due to the inception of some modern taxation systems or budgeting which was not customary at that time or for other reasons, they should have preserved the [traditional] model and its simplicity and ease.

Some are so enamoured with the name of Europe that the only desire they have is that we must become fully Europeanized, without concern for the advantages or drawbacks. They champion Europe so much that they quarrel with us, as if Europe were the locus of all that is good. Humankind and such aberration?!

It is even more peculiar that since in recent years the Iranian state has become strengthened and tax dues are obtained with ease, these [advocates], these ignorant of heart attribute it to European laws. Woe to those whose servility leads them to praise their own virtues in another's name.

If they had insight, the [comparative] assessment of Iranian and European laws would be the clearest testimony to perceive the Europeans' deviance [from reason] and their confusion. Is it not deviance to assign to one hundred persons the task that can be done by ten persons?! Is it ingenious to weave a web like spiders and to entangle the foot [i.e. complicate tasks]?!

This is not an exaggeration: many of Europe's laws are so convoluted and utterly entangled that the wretched official or person involved in legal bureaucracy becomes perplexed and cannot weave his way out.

Law is itself the medium to completing an undertaking. Thus, this medium must be direct and straightforward so too much elaboration and attention to detail is a flaw in relation to law. In most of the laws of Europe there are so many nuances that with each step there is a turn, and the traveller must pause at each turn for so long that he either forgets the destination or becomes weary and resigns halfway.

As we have said many of Europe's laws have been erected upon the principle of 'antithesis' because they were established in reaction to movements in the previous century. Since in earlier times the affairs were in the hands of an expert who completed the tasks by drawing on his own intelligence and discretion without resorting to deeds or paperwork, for this reason in these [new] laws, out of antipathy for the former system, they have assigned all affairs to bureaucracy and deeds. And they have shown such generosity in this regard that they are far removed from wisdom.

In regard to taxation laws this defect is also apparent. Every tax [detail] must be recorded in several books, wasting much paper to this end.

If such fastidiousness is for the purpose of preventing errors or fraud, Iranian bookkeeping, despite its simplicity, was immune to errors and fraud. If the purpose is to investigate a specific tax record years later through those books and papers, alas presently the reverse effect is achieved because due to the excess of paper and books it is the most difficult task to trace the trail. However, traditional accountants who are still living can still easily recover from their simple records Iran's taxes from thirty years ago. An operation must be sound; otherwise out of excessive effort and excessive tools springs forth nothing but defect.

If we are dwelling on this topic for a long time, it is because this topic is a clear example of Europism's antagonism [to the East]. Europeans speak of the East's incapacity and incompetence and impose mandates on certain regions on this pretext, [in this way] infiltrating many countries. One of their reasons for this is the lack of law in the East and that the affairs are chaotic and disorderly. In other words, the Europeans have found a political justification out of the fact that the Easterners accept Western laws across the board. We want to see how accurate this justification is, and since any argument is better illustrated through examples, we address this topic.

All we know is that Europe's claim to superiority is absurd. If a group of people invent some instruments thanks to which they raided [other regions] for some time, inflicting all manners of violence and malevolence [on others], this is not the cause of their superiority.

The claim about the East's lawlessness is also absurd. The only problem with the Easterners is their servility vis-à-vis Europe, trampling upon their own virtues and adopting their [Europeans'] vices, exchanging gold for copper.

We lament the mistakes that were made at the outset of the Constitutional Movement in the name of Europism. We hope that those past errors are put to rights now that Europe's designs have been unveiled and that, on the other hand, Iran has become strengthened and ordered.

More than anything we wish that reason is not undermined by ignorance and that our simple and beneficial laws are not trampled upon by Europism. Also [we hope that] Easterners rekindle their energy and shake off the dust of servility. In matters pertaining to right and wrong, there is no East or West. We took what was good from Europe's inventions, but at the same time let us not permit that our virtues be trampled upon by Europism so that Europe can use this same practice as a justification for its ignoble designs.

Chapter Fifteen

The laws of Europe [on jurisprudence]

A few things must also be said about Europe's judicial system. Iran had a department of justice, or an office of arbitration, since the time of the Achaemenids,[29] even before them. We find mention of it in histories, though little is known about their laws and processes of implementation. With the advent of Islam, one of the worthiest achievements of Muslims was [attention to] justice so much so that the Caliph appointed in every town a judge who had wide-ranging jurisdiction and his judgment applied to all from infant to adult.

Those familiar with Islamic history are aware of the high station of *fiqh*, which is the equivalent to the European science of law, among Muslims and of the vast knowledge acquired by the jurists [*faqihān*] and their contributions to this science in comparison to which, in many cases, the [European] science of law pales.[30]

For centuries in Iran and other Islamic countries the best judicial system was in currency. The judge was appointed on account of [possessing] qualities rarely found in others; every dispute was resolved in one or two sittings and the verdict was executed with ease and facility.

Despite the existence of multitudes of people in towns and villages, the abundance of wealth and the prevalence of considerable trade and commerce

---

[29] Considered to be the first Persian empire, the Achaemenid state was founded by Cyrus the Great c. 550 BC and ruled over a vast territory until its dissolution around 329 BC.

[30] Islamic jurisprudence in various fields is collectively referred to as *fiqh*. It is equivalent to the science of law in its Western sense in that it involves human interpretation of the guidelines enshrined in a corpus such as a constitution. In the case of Islamic jurisprudence, that corpus is the divine guidelines outlined in the Sharia as revealed in the Quran and the Sunnah (the sayings and practices of Muhammad, the prophet of Islam). The divine guidelines in the Sharia are considered to be infallible (thus unchangeable) among Muslims. However, *fiqh* is changeable as it is the human interpretation of divine laws.

at that time, there was no need for more than one judge in each town, except in bigger cities where a separate judge was appointed for the followers of each of the four schools.[31]

Even after the demise of the caliphate and the [subsequent] reign of the Mongols,[32] the Islamic judicial system prevailed for centuries, until in recent centuries it was disrupted and disappeared. This was especially the case in Iran where due to the ignorance of the monarchs at that time and the state's weakness, the judicial system was in disarray for a long time, and it must be said that there was no such thing as a judicial system; people got along with each other on account of their piety and righteousness and every time a quarrel occurred between two people, it would be resolved with the mediation of relatives and neighbours.

But at the outset of the Constitutionalist Movement, even in this regard they turned to the laws of Europe and, following the Ottomans who had been deluded by Europism before us, they chose France and established a Ministry of Justice based upon the French [model]. But this law has great defects.

One of its defects is ceaseless inquests. According to what is written in the law, every dispute can be heard twice, but we see that in some cases the dispute is heard in excess of ten times. The Islamic judicial system appoints a judge on rigorous requirements but it also upholds his authority, content with one hearing and one judgment. But the legal system of Europe does not require much qualification for a judge so it does not comply with his judgment [which is why] it calls for constant investigation.

Is the Islamic system not better and more compliant with wisdom? Because just as we choose and follow the prescriptions of a knowledgeable, experienced and honest physician at the time of illness and infirmity, we can also follow the same course of action in regard to matters of property and assets. It is indeed foolish to visit many inexperienced physicians, rather than one knowledgeable and experienced physician, and to receive from each a different cure.

Some will argue: legal matters and medicine are different because in adjudication since there is a dispute between two parties, there is the fear that the judge may side with one of them, but there is no such situation in medicine.

---

[31] Reference to Islam's four canonical schools of law: Maliki, Hanafi, Shāfi'i, and Hanbali.
[32] The Abbasid Caliphate came to an end with the Mongol sack of Baghdad in 1258 CE.

We respond: if we appoint judges with the requirements laid out in Islam, this fear will be very negligible. On the other hand, endless hearings have many disadvantages which must not be forgotten because cases will be prolonged, enervating both parties, and perhaps the suit will be lost or cease to be the issue in the midst. After months or even years of a deadlock, the litigants find no outcome except waste of time and distress and regret. Justice that comes after years of agony, let there be no such justice.

Besides, it is as a result of these endless hearings that there is need for forming many tribunals in each city, and this itself is an excessive expense on the government's shoulder.

If we had access to judges of the type Islam prescribes, it would be better in order to make do with one hearing, but presently it is better to have two or three hearings so that after deliberation in a tribunal the person who is the losing side and is displeased can appeal to a higher court and request [further] inquiry. If both courts arrive at the same decision, it must be executed; otherwise the defendant's grievance can be examined in a third court whose judgment becomes binding and is implemented.

In any case, we must reduce excessive [use of] paperwork and deeds and simplify and facilitate proceedings. These legalisms which the French revolutionaries have inserted in law in their antithetical stance against their predecessors are not only futile and yield no benefit, but they also have many disadvantages and are indeed fetters placed upon the feet of judges and prosecutors. Default judgment must be abolished. If a person is in infraction of the court's summons, he must be treated as stringently as possible, not to embolden him by giving him undue respite. As well, unproductive talk and unproductive action must be avoided as much as possible. In Iran civic law has been modelled after *fiqh* which is the best body of laws. If *fiqh* were also the legal basis for determining the judge's qualities and the principles of jurisprudence, this country would have the best ministry of justice so that after some time other Islamic countries would follow suit as well. Perhaps the Europeans would follow suit, too, since we witness how unwise the legal system there is, yielding nothing except exorbitant costs for the government and great distress for the people. The senselessness of this legal system will become even more apparent when in one of the [other] countries a simple and worthy judicial system is instituted.

In such a situation the Europeans will also discover the inefficiency of their own legal system and will of necessity abandon it.

Some suppose that methods of jurisdiction are none but what we have adopted from Europe and so it is inevitable that every claim take years in the Ministry of Justice. Every time talk of this subject is raised, they point to Europe [saying] that over there litigation takes years as well.

This supposition is false because if we have a simple judicial system, each suit – even if it goes through three hearings – will not take more than two months. However, in the European system which we follow today, a series of unnecessary actions delay the proceedings and it cannot be known what the reason for these unnecessary actions is.

For instance, when the judge concludes the trial and pronounces his verdict, even though both the plaintiff and the defendant are present, the law does not recognize this proclamation of judgment and requires that the verdict be written down on a separate piece of paper, accompanied by a lengthy explanation, and delivered by an agent to the residences of the plaintiff and the defendant. This action, which postpones the proceedings for a month more or less, is repeated several times in each trial. Let the advocates of Europe explain: what is achieved by this unproductive measure?! If they find a benefit to this measure, we will mute our criticism; otherwise, they should confess that the laws of Europe are the most injudicious laws.

But the fact that in Europe every proceeding is prolonged, from this we realize the impotence and ignorance of Europe's legislators. This, however, does not mean that we disregard the defects of Europe's laws [themselves].

If we recognize someone as wise and rational, we revere him. This proselytization and reverence will last for as long as he does not commit a senseless act; otherwise we consider him unwise and do not revere him. Just because we [initially] recognized him as rational and wise, it should not mean that whatever we see him do, even if it is senseless, we will admire it.

It is the practice of fools to applaud and submit to the words and deeds of a man only because they find him externally groomed. The wise recognize the man from his deeds, not the deeds from the man. According to the Bible, a tree must be known by its fruit. If a tree, however robust and beautiful, yields acrid fruits, it must be uprooted and burned, not to disregard the acridity of its fruit due to its robustness and beauty!

At the outset of the Constitutional movement many groups of Europeans were brought to Iran with hefty expenses and trusted with the administration of government offices. These, most of whom were ignorant and uninformed people, unaware of the history and laws of this land, embarked, before anything else, upon propagating the labyrinthine laws of their own countries here. Perhaps some among them even prided themselves [on their achievement], obliging Iranians with the favour of their unwise actions.

To amend those unwise actions, today Iran can institute a series of simple and transparent laws in administration such that in a short while they win fame and throughout the East they will be followed, perhaps even the Europeans will follow suit as well. If those who have greatly promoted Europe find our assertion difficult to accept, it is not unknown to the wise that Europeans do not have legislative capacity, every law that they legislate turning out gravely senseless and unwise – as we have witnessed with our eyes – and it is best for them to abide by the laws of Easterners.

Chapter Sixteen

Good disposition and bad disposition

In regard to ethics, we do not have much dispute with Europe and do not intend to address each and every good disposition or bad disposition. We know full well that Europe has been the land of knightly chevaliers and that Christ's religion has prevailed in that region for centuries. We never deny that there are many select and worthy people among Europeans. But it must not be concealed that Europe's present-day turpitude is eradicating the foundation of good dispositions and every day the extent of bad dispositions will increase.

With irreligiosity and greed and false teachings which are Europe's current problems, the foundation of good disposition has become volatile, unless the select [among Europeans] can oppose such evils and not relinquish human dispositions.

Due to irreligiosity, a large group [of people] have violated all restraint, rejecting all mores. It is evident what disposition such individuals will display.

Perpetrators of false teachings make the most senseless assertions and blurt out the most poisonous thoughts, each trying to utter the most shocking declaration to win more fame. They have made people repulsed by humanity, calling them to follow animals. They are indeed sworn enemies of humanity and worthy character.

Finally greed: this calamity has set Europe on fire and it is indisputable that the greatest cause of Europe's destruction will be this evil. In a place where certain individuals amass millions in wealth from machines and factories without any concern for the ruination of millions of families while doing their best to thwart any attempt for a remedy; in a land where some have made the sale of military equipment their business, constantly fanning the flames of conflict in order to instigate a war and ensure demand for their goods[33]; in such a place it would be a wonder to inquire about good disposition. If beasts in mountains and deserts possess humanity and worthy qualities, so do these greed-mongers.

In the events of the war between Japan and China, we witnessed how the greedy governments of Europe did not honour the articles of the Geneva Convention forbidding the sales of military equipment to a belligerent state by not declining to sell equipment to Japan.

Is not this breach of trust and disloyalty representative of the bad disposition of Europeans?! Where governments commit such acts, what can we expect from others?!

Today in Europe thousands of companies and factories have been established for the production and sale of pharmaceuticals. Most of these do not attach the slightest value to the lives and health of people and seek nothing but amassing wealth. They allow all manners of fraud, producing some drugs, publicizing them on false claims, and distributing them throughout the East and the West with the help of like-minded physicians without any concern for the lives they destroy.[34]

In a place where certain people consider wealth as the pillar of life, audaciously speaking and writing about this ominous false teaching of theirs, inevitably such injustices are generated, smearing, in that manner, the face of humanity.

God's elect endeavoured for centuries and had cleansed the world of this blemish [i.e. amassing wealth at all costs]. Suddenly Europe tries to encourage

---

[33] Here Kasravi is describing what would in the following decades be termed the 'military-industrial complex', the growing influence within the government of private military contractors with a vested interest in promoting public policies that favour profits from weapons production and sales rather than national interest or democracy. The first person credited with having used the expression is US President Dwight D. Eisenhower in his Farewell Address on 17 January 1961. In part of his address, Eisenhower warned: 'In the councils of government, we must guard against the acquisition of unwarranted influence, whether sought or unsought, by the military industrial complex. The potential for the disastrous rise of misplaced power exists and will persist'. Military-Industrial Complex Speech, Dwight D. Eisenhower, 1961, The Avalon Project, https://avalon.law.yale.edu/20th_century/eisenhower001.asp.

[34] Like his description of the military-industrial complex, Kasravi is here describing what decades later, starting in the 1970s onward, would be termed the 'medical-industrial complex' (also known as the 'pharmaceutical-industrial complex'). Many books have been written on the subject, but its basic premise is analogous to the military-industrial complex in the United States: The corporatization of health care – through a network of doctors, hospitals, insurance companies, manufacturers of drugs and medical equipment, health consultants, banks and so on – primarily for profit.

it, singing its own praises for this foolishness. In this situation, what hope can one have of virtue from that region?!

Someone should ask: cinema, which you seek to promote so much, what benefit does it have for human life? If it is for entertainment, how does entertainment merit reverence and worldwide promotion in this manner?! How does it befit entertainment to be considered a science and have academies erected for its sake[35]?! Are these brazen displays, which breach the foundation of chastity and steer millions of women towards impurity annually, a science?! Is it not because it makes you money that you greed-mongers display so much devotion to it and utterly disregard the damages it does to the world?! Fie upon this greed-mongering, fie!

We witness with our eyes what baseness those from among Easterners who have travelled to Europe or have become European-mannered by reading books have gravitated to: they have no art except thievery and deceitfulness and shamelessness; in accordance with the principles of Darwinism they are ever after craftiness and wickedness and embark upon accumulation of possessions and self-indulgence in any way they can.

We know of physicians who have returned from Europe with greed-filled hearts who commit such wicked acts in the name of the medical profession. The medical profession was not seen as a means of amassing wealth among the Easterners. This is why physicians were not after anything but a good name. They were satisfied with the slightest remuneration from the poor and the needy while charging the wealthy no more than the care they provided. These greed-mongers have turned that [profession] into a means for pillage and plunder, employing any form of deception in the name of the medical profession.

Some individuals flaunt those scientists in Europe who made invaluable discoveries in medicine, overlooking accumulation of wealth and making their discoveries available to the public free of charge. Or they remind us of the charitable elite who have founded hospitals out of their purses of generosity. We recognize these generous men and the value of their actions. However, one swallow does not make a summer. Most of these charitable

---

[35] Kasravi is most likely referring to the founding and establishment of the Academy of Motion Pictures Arts and Sciences (AMPAS) which came into existence in the United States in May 1927.

works are by those who have not yet been tainted with irreligiosity and greed so there are still traces of those age-old good dispositions in them. At any rate, this flood of greed which has of late arisen from Europe will destroy the entire region, leaving little trace of the good deeds of the ancestors, if some wise men do not contain it.

Chapter Seventeen

The value of Europe's inventions

The purpose of these assertions is [to argue] that the life of a community is not lived through ironware. On the contrary, the foundation of life and the basis of welfare and contentment are other important things. In other words, the basis of life is not automobiles, aero planes, telegraph, telephones, radios, electricity; such things do not justify the claim: because Europeans have invented these instruments and have made accomplishments in this respect, we must abandon all we have and follow them. Rather, the basis of life and what leads people to happiness is, first, the ethos of coexistence, second law and third good dispositions, of all of which the Europeans are sorely deprived and impoverished, in the manner we have described [above] each of the three factors and revealed the Europeans' impoverishment.

The Easterners converting to the marvels of Europe and using them as a pretext for Europism are similar to some people who see a man with clean and new clothes. Based on this one good sign, they also recognize him as rich, wise, well-mannered and sincere. Or [it is like] some people assuming a person with good penmanship to also be learned and intelligent such that if he even claimed to be a doctor, they accept it from him with no justification.

If we need another example, it must be said: a man plans to travel and wishes to always be carefree and at peace. It goes without saying that the condition for realizing this wish is first the safety of the road so that thieves and highway robbers do not have access to his life and possessions by way of harm. Second, the existence of villages on the way so that he can obtain food and water and rest somewhere at night time. Third, the company of a companion so that he is not alone. This companion must be kind and honest and not betray him or [greed after] his possessions. But if he does not concern himself with these conditions and embarks on the journey solely relying upon horse and holler [for help] in the company of companions who are thirsty for his blood, treading a barren and abandoned desert which is the hiding place of thieves and highway robbers, is such a person not mad and ignorant?!

All of Europe's inventions in relation to human life do not have the same value as horse and holler in relation to the journey. And it is out of ignorance that some people close their eyes to all other aspects and instead direct their stare at these instruments.

Before anyone else, the Europeans themselves have been deceived because it is due to their mistake that they have not comprehended the meaning and value of the ethos of life, unobservant of its virtues, while they do not see the world's progress in anything except ensuing from the manufacture of tools. This is how from the day they attained inventions and created some instruments, they claimed progress and ascendancy. Not only do they not have a liking for Easterners and consider themselves superior to them, they also have no liking for their own predecessors, opening their mouths wide in their reproach and denunciation.

With the emergence of every new invention, Europe considers it a step towards the world's progress meanwhile disregarding the injustices that have appeared and spread around the world during the two centuries of Europe's resurgence.

It must be said that Europe has been deceived while it also deceives because both the politicians and capitalists of Europe have created these labels in justification of their actions and policies. All this ballyhoo about Europe's 'modern civilization' and about Europeans' supremacy which they have echoed around the world, as well as condemnation of Easterners and Eastern ways of life, are mostly for the purpose of Easterners considering their own life inferior and worthless and feeling ashamed and disgraced so that they easily accept the yoke of Western lordship on their necks.

Those who pontificate about the East in books or newspapers are mostly ignorant people who cannot distinguish between the world's benefit or harm and do not comprehend the meaning of ascendancy and superiority. But many of them are also ignoble persons who intend to strike at the splendour and magnificence of the East by doing so, thereby portraying them [i.e. the people of the East] as inferior and abject in their own eyes. Likewise, many of those who in Iran and other cities in the East have made a career out of praise for the West and constantly open their mouths wide in denouncing and reproaching Easterners, who knows if they are not paid mercenaries of Europe, seeking the destruction of the East to their [masters'] heart desire?!

How does it befit intelligent and sincere people to disregard all the virtues of the East, to wish Easterners to be averse to all the principles of decency, and to not acknowledge anything from them except Europism?! These are either ignorant persons or ignoble people.

Why must they not be aware that if Europe has had inventions and created wondrous instruments, we can adopt only those instruments but must never lose our own way of life and laws [and we can do so] without having to follow the West in these respects?! Especially since the way of life which the messengers of God have assigned to us is the best of principles. The wider its prevalence, the more tranquil people's lives will be. As well, we have access to the most simple and beneficial laws and are never in need of the West's unwise laws.

Some believe that we are more backward compared to Europe and must endeavour to reach them. This is one of the lies propagated by the policies of Europe and the ignorance of Europists. Why must a group follow others to confirm that they are behind in relation to them?! Never mind Europe, even if we walk behind African Bedouins, we will be behind in relation to them and will never reach them. But why would we do this?!

As we have said, Europe's sole achievements are its inventions, and we must adopt many of those inventions and will be behind the Westerners in this respect, until some masters from among the Easterners learn those sciences well and reach the level of Western scientists. Aside from this, in other respects, neither Europe has any achievements, nor do we have to follow it. On the contrary, as we have said many times, in regards to the ethos of coexistence, laws, and good dispositions, which are the three important pillars of life, Europe is hopelessly baffled and entangled and is itself in need of following Easterners.

Chapter Eighteen

East and West

We have said this and assert it again: we have no enmity towards Westerners. Whether Eastern or Western, we are all humans and no one has ascendancy over the other. That there are some criticisms from us towards the Westerners, these criticisms are not by way of enmity but for the purpose of the world's awakening. What will we do if we do not criticize those who seek the destruction of the world and deprive people of welfare and contentment?! A group of people who have the worst ways of life, the most senseless laws, and the ugliest of dispositions, smearing humanism and disgracing humanity, all the while boasting about their supremacy and considering others base, what kind of treatment can one give such a group of people?! Should one not enumerate each and every one of their defects and unmount them from their horse of arrogance?!

Europe is treading the path to destruction and is driving others towards destruction as well. In such a situation, can one opt for silence, or can one be anxious about the venomous disapprovals of the advocates of Europe without saying what must be said?! Whoever possesses knowledge and a good nature has the duty today not to keep silent and to endeavour to awaken the world.

We have not withheld and will not withhold [our] compassion and guidance from Westerners either. That we have supposed East and West as separate [entities] and do not speak of them in one place is because the West has its own afflictions and the East [has] its own. The former is [caught] in a trap and will not easily break out and the latter is not yet entrapped and can easily escape. This is why each must be discussed separately.

It is the Europeans' own doing to divide the world into two spheres, supposing the East and the West to be separate [entities], elevating Westerners and regarding Easterners with contempt.[36]

From the day Europeans became strong, they have sought to uproot the East, invading every region on the pretence of a civilizing mission. Wherever they landed, they have abandoned humanity and adopted ignoble Machiavellian prescriptions. They overcame the indigenous populations through pillage, deception, sedition, slaughter and fire, thereby embarking upon sucking their blood. In any country they conquered, whether in Asia or Africa, after centuries of ruling and colonizing those places, they still do not mix with the locals who are the rightful owners of that land, not considering them one of their own or themselves as one of theirs in order to alleviate their [the locals'] feeling of humiliation and inferiority.

Everywhere they only employ two methods: on the one hand, they rob the locals of their resources on continuous and various pretexts, dispatching those [earnings] to Europe meanwhile clipping their wings so that they never dream of flying untethered in the sky. On the other hand, using deception and sophistry they incite all manners of disturbance among them, preventing them from uniting and conceiving of a solution.

They do not find the Eastern way of life agreeable and compel Easterners everywhere to adopt Europism. Everywhere there must be theatres, cinemas and clubs for women and men to mingle together freely. Besides automobiles, aero planes, telegraph, telephone and the electrical lamp, all sorts of European commodities must be amply distributed, creating a favourable market for Western capitalists. Numerous schools must be opened for the purpose of squandering the lives of youngsters. Ministries of justice and finance and other such departments must be founded, modelled on the labyrinthine and unwise laws of Europe. Darwinism and other such poisonous prescriptions by the false masters of the West must be spread everywhere and indecent acts must be fostered. In every respect Europe must be followed; otherwise the people

---

[36] In his usual allusive style, Kasravi is here referring to Orientalism. As a cultural discourse, Orientalism is premised on a perceived foundational difference between "East" and "West", with the latter being essentially superior to the former. Orientalist discourse would have been at its unapologetic peak in the 1930s when Kasravi published *Ethos*.

will be disconnected from civilization and their name must be tarnished. Or control of their affairs must be seized under the label of a Mandate and they then must be entrapped.

[The Europeans scheme thus:] If a people are not weak enough for us to easily overpower, we must resort to trickery to create disturbance among them, turning them against each other, and in this way weaken them. Or we must promote Europism with the aid of some individuals from among them so that we can thus accomplish our goal [and conquer them].

We have already mentioned civilization and civility, describing their true meaning.* However, European authors, those of them who are among the learned, have distorted the original meaning, taking it [civilization] to mean literacy and the like. In their estimation we can consider a people in possession of civilization only if literacy is prevalent among them and their life is based upon knowledge. Journalists and politicians do not even honour this definition and instead consider civilization to be life with automobiles, aero planes, clubs, theatres and cinemas, in other words today's [notion of] Europism. We witness how they do not consider a people civilized unless they possess these instruments and stoop to a series of dishonourable acts. Then on the pretext of the civilizing mission, they invade their country and as soon as they prevail, they spread irreligiosity and Darwinism and other poisonous philosophies before doing anything else. On the other hand, after the indigenous population takes to Europism, establishing schools and learning European sciences, they [the colonizers] sabotage their efforts and do everything they can to prevent their progress in this undertaking so that they do not lose the pretext of the civilizational mission and can always suck the blood of those hapless people.

This is a snippet of Europe's treatment of the East. Does this treatment not deserve criticism?!

These injustices [committed] by Europe in the past few centuries, along with its own problems today, are akin to a person who has left his house dazed and drunk. On the street he swears at the first person he runs into. He taunts the second person, slaps the third, swindles the fourth. He does not withhold

---

* Chapter 12 of Part I.

his harassment from anyone he runs into. Since he does not watch where he is treading out of drunkenness, he loses his way and falls into a swamp. Instead of going back and dislodging himself, he continues to tread on, thus sinking further into the mud. Who knows if he will be delivered from this entrapment or if he will perish under the mud due to his injustices.

Chapter Nineteen

The Great Geneva Conventions

We have made mention of Europe's problems in the proper place. What must be said here is that these problems will not easily be solved. On the contrary, if conditions remain what they are today, what will not lead to a solution are Europe's problems.

The noisy fuss they make, the solutions they propose, the conferences and councils they continuously hold, the messages and proposals which news agencies broadcast, if some count on these actions [as a solution], we know full well that these are all out of utter desperation. They take these measures to make work; they display them to conceal their helplessness.

After several years, what has all the talk about reduction in arms accomplished?! Or what resulted from the world economic conference?![37]

The weightiest institution in Europe is the Geneva Conventions which after fifteen years of high hopes during the events of the Sino-Japanese war revealed its inefficiency. After eighteen months of deliberation, what assistance did they give the injured plaintiff, China, and what retribution to the aggressor, Japan?!

The Conventions' charter, under Article Sixteen, provides that in such a situation member states should before anything else sever all commercial and friendly ties with the aggressor state, compelling other governments to also cut ties. They should then form a military alliance to subjugate the belligerent state. It must be asked: how did they not take those measures in regards to Japan?!

A greedy oppressor finds his neighbour weak and seizes his house from him. They go to the judge for arbitration. After investigation, [the judge] rules that the greedy must cease taking the house. But he does not obey the ruling and

---

[37] Most likely a reference to the London Economic Conference of 1933 attended by representatives of 66 nations in order to revive global economy after the Great Depression. The seeds of the London Conference were planted in 1931 when US President Herbert Hoover called for an international conference to address global economic recovery.

objects. The judge dismisses both and relieves himself of the headache. When they exit, the aggressor, out of spite for the suit, begins to beat up the neighbour and takes all of his clothes too. What sense is there in such judgment?! A judge who does not enforce his own ruling, wondrous is his judgment!

Based on what we have experienced and know for certain, Westerners for centuries set aside wisdom and achieved their goals through coercion, deception and oppression so often that they have become disconnected from wisdom and estranged to the ethos of humanity. This is why they are helpless in overcoming the difficulties they face today, problems that will not be alleviated without the assistance of wisdom and by means of the ethos of humanity.

Every time they devise a plan and after trials they find out that it was useless so they devise another plan. What benefit has resulted from all those conferences, commissions and associations?! Why is it that the more they try, the more caught up they are?! Why do they not understand that every problem has a cause and unless the cause is removed, yet another plan is like flogging a dead horse?!

This is like a blind person who walks through a dead-end alleyway: he will not realize his mistake until he hits the wall. What is worse is, first, when Europeans revel at [being at] the head of that alleyway, praising themselves and condescending to others, and, second, when they hit the wall and turn back.

What is more detrimental than anything are the hidden motives disguised as [sincere] solutions. In every situation what the governments claim or pretend is not what they genuinely intend. This is why they are always wary of each other and can never cooperate to achieve a goal.

If there were no hidden motives, during the Sino-Japanese affair the Geneva Convention should have implemented Article Sixteen and confronted Japan by any means possible in order to discipline Japan into understanding its limits. By doing so, the Convention would have earned respect and its status would have been elevated; afterwards no government would needlessly instigate aggression and peace would prevail everywhere.

But at the present time the Convention has lost all respect and everyone knows that vis-à-vis a belligerent state it is incapable of doing anything except providing verbal empathy! If this is Europe's weightiest institution, proving to be so ineffective and unwise, what hope can one have of Europeans' other undertakings?!

Chapter Twenty

What is our argument?

In brief, our argument is that Europe's claim to progress and supremacy is an outright deception. The world will not find progress and ascendancy in some inventions or discoveries in some sciences. Easterners who are enamoured by the West's wondrous deeds and believe its claim to progress and ascendancy, stimulated into action everywhere and running after it [Europe], they have also been utterly deceived.

If we seek the truth, Europe has tended towards baseness and backwardness in the past few centuries and is terribly entangled. Easterners who are unwisely following in its footsteps are hastening towards entanglement with their own feet.

Most of the Westerners' actions are dissociated from wisdom and inconsistent with the ethos of humanity. Those instances of war and virulent aggression, the crimes of [its] politicians, that rapacious mercantilism and profiteering, those false indoctrinations and irreligiosity, those labyrinthine and senseless laws, the disruption of life's balance, that Bolshevism and starvation among the Russians – which of these conforms to wisdom or corresponds to the ethos of humanity?!

What was the bloody war of 1914 for and what came out of it?! Some claim: wars have always occurred everywhere. We respond: every deed, whether good or bad, must be for a specific purpose. What was the purpose of that war?! The Germans who initiated that war and slaughter and whose madness amounted to breaking the terms of the treaty they had signed with [other] governments, using poisonous gases, what benefits were they hoping to gain?! Even if they were victorious, what would be the outcome?! What benefits did the others who became victorious gain?! Were these actions guided by wisdom?!

The misdeed that the politicians allow in their profession, is it in accordance with the ethos of humanity?! Why on earth are all manners of wickedness allowed in this field?! What important feats are they accomplishing that justifies their outright violation of the ethos of humanity?! Was the world not faring well before the appearance of these bloodthirsty predators?! Governance or guardianship of the world does not call for such wickedness. These are all the consequence of the animosity existing among the peoples of Europe because of which they have been thirsting for each other's blood and allowing all manners of baseness for the purpose of domination over each other. It is utterly against wisdom and humanity for two groups to take animosity to this level. For as long as the world has existed, it has not witnessed such wickedness and immorality from humans. It is even more despicable that the Europeans have clothed such inhumanity in the garb of patriotism and do as they do with impudence.

Trade and business, as we have said, are means for the progress of the world's affairs, but people's welfare and contentment must always be valued more than those [trade and business]. However, the Europeans value business more than human life, manufacturing and weaving not to produce useful items in people's lives but in order to sell and accumulate capital. It has gotten to the point where governments, which must be guardians of people, have forgotten their duty and solely turned to the support of businesspeople and factory owners. They have taken their interest in trade and business to such a level that they do not even stop at [instigating] wars and massacre in its fulfilment, and they [even] speak and write about this folly with impudence. More curiously, they laugh at forebears and ancients who did not recognize trade as such, considering themselves superior to them [forebears]. Woe to this folly, woe!

If wisdom were a consideration, they would realize from the outset that this type of rapacious mercantilism has no outcome except ruination and destruction. If they were not blind to wisdom, they would learn a lesson from their current state and would realize what the outcome of their action is. America which is the centre of this brand of rapacious mercantilism and has had the largest factories for long years, exporting goods the world over, what condition is it in currently?! On the one hand, there are eleven million unemployed and large cities are filled with vagabond and homeless children. On the other hand, there are the greedy who have closed the doors of sustenance upon those ill-fated people and utterly ruined them, and they [the ill-fated people], in turn, lament their wretched state.

[This situation is] similar to a group of bandits who at times of anarchy lurk in the shadows of a cave and every day raid a village, looting the belongings of the inhabitants and utterly ruining thousands of families without sparing anyone. For years they indulge themselves in this manner, thinking that this is the only way the world should be. They launch into boasting about their superiority and ascendancy, denouncing their own forefathers and those virtuous men who earn sustenance through their own efforts and labour and considering themselves superior to them. This continues until all the villages are looted and left in ruins and there is nothing left to plunder, or some villages resolve to defend themselves, entrenching themselves against their incursion. It is at this time that the noose tightens around the bandits' necks, or in the words of Westerners, an 'economic crisis' takes place. Then they start to whine about unfavourable conditions and every day think of a remedy and every time seek a new solution. But every plan they hatch is thwarted and finally they all perish, or they are compelled to abandon banditry and return to their forefathers' upright way of life.

This analogy is not an exaggeration. The West's idea of business is nothing but banditry, and the efforts of Europe and America today in the name of a cure for the crisis are nothing but bandits' schemes. Sometimes they see the solution in weaving or producing flimsy goods so that they malfunction after a short while, driving people to more consumption. They do not comprehend that even if this dishonesty has a favourable impact, it will not last longer than a while. And then if all tradespeople also follow this dishonest policy, what condition will the world be in?! At other times they plan to devalue their currency, not understanding that this is nothing but reducing the price of [export] goods, which will not have a long-lasting effect. They boast about being clever but do as children and lunatics do.

If wisdom were a consideration and some people could distinguish benefit from harm, it would seem self-explanatory that to be delivered from the West's present twisted state, trade and craftsmanship must be restored to their traditional ways. They must manufacture or weave what people need to manage life's affairs, and to manufacture or weave them according to the people's need. Likewise, to be relieved of the problem of unemployment, they must reduce the abundance of machines.

Otherwise in a place where the affluent erect factories, activate enormous machines and seek avariciously to accumulate wealth, there will be no outcome except, on the one hand, the closing of the means of sustenance to thousands, even millions, of families who will be reduced to beggary and, on the other, the manufacturing or weaving, then amassing, of excessive tools or fabric so that they are forced to think of alternative ways to sell them. And when they cannot find an alternative that is in accordance with the ethos of humanity, of necessity they resort to deceit and dishonesty, as is the case today with the West.

In a place where folly and baseness have become so commonplace that some people produce medicine, not to meet the needs of the ill, but for the purpose of sales and accumulation of capital in any way possible, can one look for wisdom and humanity in such a place?!

Taking flight in the sky, penetrating into the depths of the sea, hearing each other's words from hundreds of miles away, and other such feats which are the result of Europe's inventions, can these redeem those instances of baseness and folly?!

While the West is in this condition, the Easterners consider it to be in a state of progress and ascendancy and follow in its steps, their sole dream being to reach its state. Pity on such folly, pity!

The world today is misguided. The world has left behind the path of salvation and scrambles in the desert of misguidance, foolishly not cognizant of its own state and [instead] speaking of salvation. Today more than anytime the world is in need of a guide. There is need for a man of God to reveal the path to the world and to lead the inhabitants of the world to the path of redemption.

Men of God have always redirected the world from the path of misguidance. Today, also, deliverance will be in the hands of none other than a man of God. Otherwise if left to others, they can only bring the world to where Europe is today. Despite all their wondrous progress in sciences and the abundance of scientists, and despite all the boast about philosophy, they are entrapped in such fashion. This itself is testimony to the fact that nothing springs forth from those sciences than harm and increased misguidance. The ethos of human life must be ordained by men of God, and those noble men must reveal the path to salvation.

Humans are of the same essence as animals and carry many animal traits in their nature. This is why human existence is like a road that has wisdom and humanity at one end and animal disposition at the other. Each human being sometimes makes progress towards wisdom and humanity and sometimes moves backward and tends towards animal disposition. From the outset it was the divine mentors who taught the inhabitants of the world lessons about humanity, prompting them to conform to wisdom. Otherwise, if left to themselves, humans will turn back and gravitate towards animal disposition.

In similar fashion, today Europe is utterly detached from wisdom and humanity. Greed, animosity, bloodthirstiness, deception and lack of compassion, which are the basis of Westerners' way of life, are the temperaments of beasts and cattle.

The Easterners who are following in Europe's footsteps will soon be afflicted with those temperaments, far detached from humanity. This is why there is need for the rise of some guides to direct the inhabitants of the world away from backward movement and from gravitating towards baseness and to lead them to the path of wisdom and humanity.

Afterword

Āʿin: A defining text in Ahmad Kasravi's œuvre

Stanisław Adam Jaśkowski

Kasravi – One man, many myths

Ahmad Kasravi (1890–1946) is generally considered among the most influential Iranian scholars and intellectuals. Coming from a conservative family in the northwestern city of Tabriz, he received seminary education as a young man. A brilliant autodidact, he dabbled in modern sciences and went on to become a successful scholar, especially in the field of history. As for his professional career, in the late 1910s/early 1920s he joined the newly formed modern Judiciary, leaving it after around ten years to pursue his social and religious calling, all the while supporting himself from his work as a defence lawyer.

As a testament to his scholarship, his *Shahryārān-e Gomnām* ('Forgotten Rulers'), *Tārikh-e Pānsad-Sāleh-ye Khuzestān* ('Five-Hundred-Years' History of Khuzestan') and finally his monumental work on the history of the Constitutional Revolution have long been milestones in Iranian historiography. Still, he is even better known for his opposition to Sufism and classical Persian literature, going as far, in his later years, as burning 'corrupting' books – mostly in these categories, but not limited to them – in a ritual called *Ketābsuzān* ('Book burning'), celebrated on the first day of winter. Kasravi's rationale for burning books was to destroy the medium through which harmful ideas could spread, hence the ceremonies were accompanied by lectures or sermons on the harms done by the said books and ideas.[1]

---

[1] While it is hard to pin-point the exact timespan of the book-burnings, they became especially popular in the 1940s. For a record of such ceremonies, see: A. Kasravi, *Yekom-e Dey* ('First of Dey', i.e. the first winter month of the Iranian calendar), 1322 (1943) and A. Kasravi, 'Yekom-e Deymāh va Dāstānash', *Parcham* 1, no. 1 (1943): 2–7, no. 3 (1943): 100–102. A discussion of the practice can also be found in Stanisław Adam Jaśkowski, *Parcham: Journal of Ahmad Kasravi and*

Conversely, Kasravi also holds an imagined status as the embodiment of a staunch nationalist, rejecting everything foreign, and opposed to everything non-Iranian,[2] sometimes with the appended caveat that compared to the other Iranian nationalists of the late nineteenth and early twentieth century he was not entirely anti-Islamic.[3] Of course, these voices ignore Kasravi's well-established participation in the Arabic literary and cultural life: a number of his – especially early – works were published in Arabic[4] and he himself had no problem spending time with the Arabs.[5]

Probably the most enduring perception of Kasravi, however, has been his opposition to clericalism and certain aspects of Shiite religiosity and Shiism in general. Reinforced by his assassination at the hands of the militant Shiite group Fadā'iyān-e Eslām ('The Devotees of Islam'), his popular image is that of a progressive intellectual killed by the reactionary, clerical forces. This became even more imprinted in the public imagination following the *fatwa* calling for the death of Salman Rushdie for insulting Islam. Given that Ayatollah Ruhollah Khomeini who issued the *fatwa* had previously attacked Kasravi,[6] it became tempting to connect the two.[7]

Thus, it is clear that Ahmad Kasravi, the man taken as the entirety of his ideas, was a figure with many faces. The one which seems to have dominated public imagination – that of a secular intellectual – is not only incorrect, it is in complete contrast to Kasravi's ideas broadly considered.

An example of a more sophisticated variant of this misconception appears in Jalal Al-e Ahmad's (1923–1969) seminal *Dar Khedmat va Khiyānat-e*

His Followers: A Snapshot from the History of Press in Iran (Warszawa: Wydawnictwo Akademickie Dialog, 2017), 68–77. An overview of Kasravi's criticism of classical literature can be found in Jazayery, Mohammad Ali, 'Ahmad Kasravi and the Controversy over Persian Poetry. 1. Kasravi's Analysis of Persian Poetry', IJMES 4, no. 2 (1973): 190–203, and a less sympathetic analysis in Lloyd Ridgeon, *Sufi Castigator* (London: Routledge, 2006), 45–63, 137–59.

[2] 'Abd al-Nabi Qayyem, *Pānsad Sāl Tārikh-e Khuzestān*, (Tehran: Akhtaran, 1388/2009–10), 43–53.

[3] Cf. 'Abd al-Nabi Qayyem, *Pānsad Sāl Tārikh-e Khuzestān*, (Tehran: Akhtaran, 1388/2009–10), 46–7, 52–3.

[4] Cf. Mahmud Katirā'i, 'Ketābshenāsi-ye Kasravi' ('Bibliography of Kasravi'), *Farhang-e Irān Zamin* 17 (1350 (1971–2)): 365–98. Kasravi's *Tārikh-e Hejdah-Sāleh-ye Āzarbāyjān* ('Eighteen-Years' History of Azerbaijan') was originally published in an abridged, Arabic version: Ahmad Kasravi Tabrizi, *Tārikh-e Hejdah Sāleh-ye Āzarbāyjān* (Tehran: Matba'eh-ye Mehr, Tehran 1313 (*sic*.) (1934–5)), 3.

[5] For example: Ahmad Kasravi and Mohammad Amini, *Zendegi va Zamāneh-ye Ahmad-e Kasravi/ Life and Time of Ahmad Kasravi* (Los Angeles: Ketab Corp., 2016), 341–3.

[6] Ruhollah Khomeini, *Kashf-e Asrār* ('The Unveiling of Secrets'), n.d., 10, 59–60, 332–4.

[7] For the discussion of Kasravi's assassination and its similarities with Rushdie's case see: Nasser Pakdaman, *Qatl-e Kasravi* ('Assassination of Kasravi'), 3rd ed. (Cologne: Forough Book, 2004).

Rowshanfekrān ('The Services and Disservices of the Intellectuals'), one of the chief works of the Iranian leftist intellectual, famous for his criticism of infatuation with the West and other supposed errors of the Iranian intelligentsia. Praising Kasravi's scholarly work, Al-e Ahmad accused him of being an enemy of religion, and argued that the intellectuals' opposition to religion – a movement supposedly championed by Kasravi – was what deprived the religious conservatives from receiving proper education. This, in turn, supposedly led to Kasravi's assassination. This is incorrect on two levels. First of all, Navab Safavi, the founder of Fadā'iyān-e Eslām and the mastermind behind the killing of Kasravi, had received some education – both religious and technical. Secondly, the younger Kasravi did not necessarily share his older self's attitude towards the Shiite faith, as will be demonstrated below. Similarly, it will become evident that the early Kasravi championed the local traditions and religion as opposed to Western ideas. Moreover, Al-e Ahmad incorrectly suggests that the lack of censorship against Kasravi's periodicals in the period of Reza Shah Pahlavi (r. 1925–41) – supposedly as an element of Reza Shah's modernist, anti-clerical politics – led Kasravi to create a supposed religious cult akin – in Al-e Ahmad's opinion – to the Baha'i faith.[8] This is disproven by Kasravi's being targeted by the authorities, including censorship, on a number of occasions, albeit mostly after the fall of Reza Shah.[9]

Yet even those who dismiss the secular-nationalist image of Kasravi often succumb to another misconception, which is to extrapolate the views and statements Kasravi made towards the end of his life to the entirety of his career. This pitfall is especially hard to evade, as most information about Kasravi's life comes from his autobiography, *Zendegāni-ye Man* ('My Life'), which he began publishing in 1943. It was in that period, which followed the fall of Reza

---

[8] Kasravi was a staunch opponent of the Bahā'is. See Ahmad Kasravi, *Bahā'igari*, n.d.; Stanisław Adam Jaśkowski, *Parcham: Journal of Ahmad Kasravi and His Followers: A Snapshot from the History of Press in Iran* (Warszawa: Wydawnictwo Akademickie Dialog, 2017), 85–91; Ahmad Kasravi and Mohammad Amini, *Zendegi va Zamāneh-ye Ahmad-e Kasravi/ Life and Time of Ahmad Kasravi* (Los Angeles: Ketab Corp., 2016), 111–16, 128–34, 196–203, and countless articles in Kasravi's journals. Bahā'i faith itself is a syncretic religion tracing its roots to the nineteenth-century Iran, rejected by mainstream Shiism as heretical.

[9] Stanisław Adam Jaśkowski, *Parcham: Journal of Ahmad Kasravi and His Followers: A Snapshot from the History of Press in Iran* (Warszawa: Wydawnictwo Akademickie Dialog, 2017), 37–9; 'Goftār-e Āqā-ye Soltānzādeh' ('The Speech of Mr. Soltānzādeh'), *Yekom-e Āzar* 1322 (1943): 23–4; Jalal Al-e Ahmad, *Dar Khedmat va Khiyānat-e Rowshanfekrān*, vol. 2 (Tehran: Khʷārazmi, 1357 (1978–9)), 157–8.

Shah and the Allied occupation of Persia, that Kasravi's views found their most radical expression, and he became the most outspoken critic of virtually the entirety of Iranian society of his time, apart from his circle of followers. His radicalism, however, was not unheard of at the time. The fall of Reza Shah's authoritarian, albeit modernist state, and the arrival of the Allied occupation forces, ushered in the wartime shortage of supplies, chaos in the political arena and ideological struggle, as well as violence and radicalism. Bahā'is were being attacked; 'modern' bathhouses, fitted with showers, were being dismantled in a conservative backlash and replaced with traditional water basins. Amidst these struggles, Kasravi's followers, standing out from the rest of society, were among the targeted groups. This led his younger disciples to organize themselves in groups to guard their meeting places, although sometimes they would physically attack those insulting Kasravi. A monument of Kasravi's thought in the period is *Varjāvand Bonyād* ('Sacred Foundation'), written in a heavily modified Persian he created for the new society he envisioned for Iran. It was the time when Kasravi was to his followers more than a scholar or a teacher – he was a divinely inspired person (*barangikhteh*).

Misconceptions about Kasravi's early years: Towards Ā'in

These circumstances of Kasravi's later years suggest that one should not uncritically accept the statements he made at that juncture. This is not to accuse him of distorting facts on purpose, as Kasravi openly admitted that before he stepped on his path of 'Pure Religiosity' (*Pākdini*),[10] he was not free of the usual vices of his contemporaries, such as smoking opium during social gatherings.[11] Having become a religious leader, however, it was only natural that he would see earlier developments in his life as leading to that point. This in turn distorted even his chronology of past events, as evident in – for example – his account of the Halley Comet and its influence on his life. Kasravi places the Comet's appearance, which led to his interest in the modern sciences, after his forced return to the clerical job: the former occurring in the

---

[10] A deistic religious movement he created through the 1930s and 1940s.
[11] 'Goftār-e Āqā-ye Kasravi' ('The Speech of Mr. Kasravi'), *Yekom-e Āzar*, 1323 (1944): 58–9.

summer of 1911, and the latter ca. September 6 of the previous year.[12] Yet the Comet arrived in the spring of 1910, before his return to the mosque. However, the version he recollected offered Kasravi a more elegant periodization of his lifetime.

Similarly, while he never concealed his early involvement with the abovementioned vices before stepping on to his new path – read: his religious revival – his later works suggest that he then had an epiphany and was no longer the same man as before. In a speech to his followers – called the Āzādegān[13] – Kasravi presented how he found himself on this new path: in 1928[14] he felt like a different man; he kept away from other people, spoke little, and spent most of his time lost in thought. Witnessing the richness of nature, he was shocked that having a cornucopia at its disposal, humanity did not live in prosperity. His emotions became volatile: he would cry, seeing a child crying; passing next to the butcher's, he would feel as if the sheep were asking him for deliverance from the tyranny of men. Seeing sparrows being sold, he was terrified that men were hunting tiny birds which could not satisfy a single person's hunger. Thus, Kasravi bought all the birds and set them free. It was since that time that he could no longer eat meat, nor even smell it.[15] He even wanted to run away from the city. Finally, he came to the conclusion that some kind of force was inspiring him to do something for the world.

Yet he saw obstacles. The path that he would set on was a path of religion which, after the scientific developments of recent centuries, had lost its former power and had gone underground. Moreover, Reza Shah, faced with the clerical opposition to his modernist reforms, turned against the mullahs and religion.

---

[12] Ahmad Kasravi and Mohammad Amini, *Zendegi va Zamāneh-ye Ahmad-e Kasravi/ Life and Time of Ahmad Kasravi* (Los Angeles: Ketab Corp., 2016), 82–3, 85–90.

[13] Plural form of *Āzādeh*, which means 'free [man]', 'freedom-loving [man]', especially referring to a person possessing the qualities a free and noble person should have. The term had also been used to mean 'Iranian'. In this context it means the followers of Pākdini who were also active in the Society (or: Party) of Āzādegān (*Bāhamād-e Āzādegān*). See: Stanisław Adam Jaśkowski, *Parcham: Journal of Ahmad Kasravi and His Followers: A Snapshot from the History of Press in Iran* (Warszawa: Wydawnictwo Akademickie Dialog, 2017), 45–58, 160–78.

[14] Ahmad Kasravi and Mohammad Amini, *Zendegi va Zamāneh-ye Ahmad-e Kasravi/ Life and Time of Ahmad Kasravi* (Los Angeles: Ketab Corp., 2016), 446; 'Goftār-e Āqā-ye Kasravi,' *Yekom-e Āzar* 1322 (1943): 13. It was the time when Kasravi temporarily quit the Judiciary.

[15] This should not be taken at face value: when he was arrested with his followers in 1942, a person was sent to bring them rice with grilled meat. It is likely that Kasravi ate only rice, but it casts doubt on his claims regarding the smell of meat. See Ahmad Kasravi, 'Yekom-e Deymāh va Dāstānash (4)' ('First of *Dey* and Its Story'), *Parcham* 1, no. 4 (1943): 148.

Thus, many opportunistic people were professing lack of faith, including some of the clerics, who would abandon their vocation for different pursuits. Some authors went as far as writing satirical poems about the prophets.

Kasravi was afraid that with the progress of sciences, religion no longer had any role to play. He dwelled on these thoughts for months, looking for an answer to the tide of irreligiosity, until he stumbled upon the answers he was looking for.

His acquaintance, 'Abdollah Negahban, having come back from America, published a booklet praising the American way of life, and sent it to Kasravi. But for Kasravi, these praises sounded more like accusations. He recalled one sentence as especially damning: 'In America time has its price, the people have no opportunity to greet each other, man and woman, big and small, strive day and night, six-year-old kids sell newspapers …'. For Kasravi this meant that life in America was filled with hardships and its people had forgotten what is truly valuable in life.

Yet in those days it was common for Iranians to look up to the West; those who came back from Europe or America would praise the foreign way of life, and these praises would echo throughout the society. But according to Kasravi, they were all wrong.

He himself was astonished that only now he discovered how they all erred, and that he did not see such a clear truth before. Whatever was the reason for this change, he thought, something had to be done. He had the answers he was looking for: religion allowed us to discover things hidden from the sciences; it still had an important role to play. In his head, he heard the answers: 'Behind the sciences, there is a series of very valuable truths' and 'It is the very sciences that led Europe astray'.[16] He felt that a veil had been lifted from his eyes. Still, he wondered how he could bring these truths to the people. He found out, however, that it did not require any force: as the people are naturally truth-seekers, if the truths are revealed, wise and pure people flock to them. Still, Kasravi was afraid that he would not be able to successfully follow his new calling; especially as he was afraid that he may succumb to temptations along the way. Finally, after around three years Kasravi made up his mind and set on this new path. First, he published *Ā'in* (Ethos), and the next year he began publishing the journal *Peymān*.[17]

---

[16] 'Goftār-e Āqā-ye Kasravi' 1322 (1943): 15–16.
[17] Ibidem, 13–16.

Era of Ā'in (Ethos)

This was how the 'late' Kasravi saw his path. While Ā'in is very prominently featured in it, it would, in Kasravi's eyes, later have to give its place as his chief religious and social treatise to other works. He himself considered Ā'in to be 'the forerunner (or herald) of Peymān' (pishrow-e Peymān), and it was the publication of the journal's first issue that would come to be celebrated by his followers as the birth of Kasravi's movement. In his journals, Kasravi would state that he was not going to reprint Ā'in, as his complete teachings could be found in Varjāvand Bonyād. He argued that in his effort to change the world he was trying to progress gradually, thus his earlier works – published before Bonyād – were incomplete; thus, publishing them again would make it possible to appreciate only their historical importance, not their actual contents.[18]

Yet, despite these comments by Kasravi, one should consider Ā'in as his most important social and religious work, not just the first. The importance of Ā'in for Kasravi's work – apart from the value of his observations on modernity and Western expansionism – lies in its being the best dispeller of the misconceptions about Kasravi and his work. Read with his other works, it even allows us to evade the pitfall of projecting the views of 'late' Kasravi on the entirety of his life.

As for the misconception of Kasravi as a Western-leaning intellectual, this myth is dispelled as soon as one even glances at Ā'in. While the Iranian criticism of the so-called *gharbzadegi* ('Westoxication'), or the irrational love of all things Western, is usually linked with Jalal Al-e Ahmad and Ahmad Fardid (1910–94), Kasravi's work could be considered the pioneering text critical of this phenomenon. Kasravi did not criticize just the Iranians blindly following the West – a phenomenon he called Europism (*urupāgari*, especially in Book 1:10). In this regard, he would not be the first to criticize, as he was preceded by, among others, the late-nineteenth-century satirical dialogue *Sheykh va Shukh* ('The Cleric and the Jester'),[19] ridiculing the superficial implementation

---

[18] 'Cherā Ā'in Rā Dobāreh Chāp Nemikonim?' ('Why Are We Not Reprinting *Ethos*'), *Parcham* 1, no. 4 (May 1943): 180.

[19] Published: Ahmad Mojāhed, ed., *Sheykh va Shukh* (Tehran: Rowzaneh, 1373). I consulted the following manuscript: Mirzā Āqā Khān Kermāni (misattribution), 'Sheykh va Shukh' (Friday, Rabi' al-Sāni/ 3 Jowzā Quy Yil 1325 (May 24 1907)), 17235, Library, Museum and Documents Center Islamic Consultative Assembly.

of European-style education and the low intellectual and moral class of the alumni and instructors of the *Dār al-Fonun*, the first Western-style polytechnic established in Iran in 1851. What gave Kasravi's criticism importance was that his rejection of the West was not a simple declaration of the superiority of local traditions, be it intellectual or religious. On the contrary, he looked for the roots of the West's crisis, and – believing that he had found them – offered a solution.

Criticizing the West, he stated that 'Europe Uproots the World's Tranquility' (title of Book 1:5). For him, the undeniable technological and scientific progress of the West did not lead to the people necessarily living happier lives. On the contrary, it led to war and destruction, as it paved the way for social Darwinism, generally identified by Kasravi, especially later, with materialism (*māddigari*). Seeing the world as an arena of war and competition, the Western powers were utilizing the instruments given to them by the scientific and technological progress without caring for their social impact. Industrial machinery, instead of satisfying people's needs and improving general prosperity, led to unemployment, the market being overflown with goods nobody could buy and crisis. Even worse, industrialization had led to the Great War, as the economic competition between the great powers turned into military conflict (Book 1:7–8).

Seeing the over-supply of the market Kasravi turned his criticism to its supposed remedy, which was modern consumerism. His words on the subject, after a few stylistic changes, could very well be uttered by a present-day activist:

> Many of the garments and toiletry or other things which we use today, [we use them] not because they have use in our life, but it is because the European factory which manufactures them finds ways to convince us to wear and apply them (…)
>
> Note Europe's infatuation with commerce; it has reached such a level that one of the affluent persons there has said that factories must make weak and flimsy products so that they quickly wear out and break, in this way amassing more capital so that the factories can continue to operate! (Book 1:7).

For Kasravi, the answer to the problem was religion. This did not mean that he was a simple moralist, preaching the virtues of austerity, personal responsibility and the return to traditional values. He not only juxtaposed the teachings of the prophets of old with the new, Western way of life, he praised traditional Eastern (Islamic) virtues, such as hospitality, charity and solidarity, which, in his opinion, were being superseded by the corrupt Western ideas (Book 1:9, 11). He went further and introduced two vital ideas.

First of all, far from requiring simple personal moral conduct, he recognized the necessity of systemic changes. While he did not state this explicitly, the reasoning here seems clear from his conclusions. A single person, after all, could not reject the harmful aspects of modern technology – in the social Darwinist world such a person would perish, not being able to compete with the industrialized superpowers. At the same time, when adopted universally, the technological advancements in practice benefitted nobody, as the increased production, speed of travel etc. impacted everyone – including all of one's rivals. This in turn led the rich to try to keep all the fruits of progress for themselves (Book 1:3).

Thus, systemic change, in Kasravi's opinion, was not simply to reject the West and isolate oneself from it – although this could be an early solution. Still, the complex change – the return to the more humane life, one which focused on human beings instead of personal wealth – had to involve humanity as a whole (Book 2:17–20).

Here comes the second way in which Kasravi's work preceded its time. In a period when Iranian intellectuals were enamoured with the West, and the slogans of the white man's burden and bringing civilization to the supposedly barbaric non-Europeans were still echoing throughout the world, he made a subversive, revolutionary claim: it was the very condition of contemporary Europe that was barbaric. Civilization, after all, was the people's ability to live together in a communal society. Hence, the great lawgivers of history – which was how Kasravi saw the prophets – laid the foundations for harmonious social life. Europeans, by rejecting religion, rejected these laws and rules, instead opting for the life of constant struggle for survival among hostile people – which is the life of animals and prehistoric humans. Hence, the Europeans were rejecting civilization, while the nations of the East were still to some degree civilized – although they were already turning to European barbarism (Book 1:12).

The solution was religion. Not religion understood as a system of dogmas and rituals, but as an ethos (*ā'in*, hence the title of the work) of coexistence, focused on helping humankind live in peace and prosperity – in short, to live like human beings should, not like wild, predatory animals (Book 1:17–18). What had to be done was to teach the entirety of mankind the proper way of life as brothers (Book 2:11, 20), and to focus the economy on fulfilling the actual needs of humankind, not on enriching the few (Book 2:12).

Hence, it is wrong to see Kasravi as a *gharbzadeh* intellectual blindly infatuated with the West – especially as his criticism of materialism would become even harsher in his later years, although it would be voiced less often. Similarly, his calls for all the downtrodden nations of the East to unite against the West's influence to a degree dispel the view of Kasravi as a radical, xenophobic nationalist. However, *Ā'in* can be a cure for another type of misconception that has been hinted at – the misconception coming from a reading of some of his later works, in which Kasravi adopts the role of a strict religious leader.

To understand this, one has to see *Ā'in* as the foundational text of Kasravi's early social and religious outlook so much so that some of his later work reads as an extension of *Ā'in*. This is particularly evident in the early issues of *Peymān* where copious references to and quotations from *Ā'in* resemble referencing a revered manifesto or holy scripture. Furthermore, this relationship between the book and the journal is supported by the titles of Kasravi's works – *Ā'in*, apart from 'Ethos', can also mean 'the Creed' or 'Law', while *Peymān* means 'a Covenant' or 'Pact' – a covenant centred around the ethos of divine creed, or divine law, as manifested in religion. Moreover, early *Peymān* focused on the same issues as those that constituted the main body of *Ā'in* – the folly of the West and the need to support the nations of the East. When the West was praised, it was when it was not the machine builder but when it was humane, god fearing, and supportive of the struggle of the oppressed. This is visible in Kasravi's review of the Persian translation of Will Durant's *The Case for India*,[20] where he describes the book's author: 'The author of this book is from America. Not from the machine-building and avaricious America, but from Christian and freedom-worshipping America'.[21]

---

[20] Published as *Ekhtenāq-e Hendustān* ('The Strangling of India').
[21] Ahmad Kasravi, 'Ketābhā. 1 – Ekhtenāq-e Hendustān,' *Peymān* 1, no. 1 (November 1, 1312): 30.

For the machine-building West, Kasravi had contempt, and entire sections of the journal were dedicated to its criticism.

Still, one has to remember that Ā'in was not in its entirety a socially progressive text – especially with regard to the ideas which at the time were identified as Western or non-Islamic. For example, it explicitly argued for a clear division between the male and female roles in society (Book 1:14). Some modern scholars argue that Kasravi later changed his views on the subject and became a supporter of women's rights – for example, this seems to be the position of Mohammad Amini, author of authoritative Persian critical editions of Kasravi's works.[22] Even he, however, failed to notice that the 'old' Kasravi still objected to female membership in the governing bodies, arguing that they should play different roles in society than men, and their education and careers should be focused on the duties traditionally seen as feminine.[23] Apart from showing another facet of Kasravi's criticism of the West, it also reminds us that there was some degree of consistency in Kasravi's views throughout his intellectual career.

Moving away from Ā'in

As time went on, however, Kasravi turned his criticism to subjects other than the West. He was especially vocal when targeting local intellectual traditions. An example here may be a comparison of his treatment of Islamic philosophy. In his earlier years – after the supposed epiphany, but before the publication of Ā'in – he praised, for example, the early modern mystic philosopher Molla Sadra (1572–1640) as a great scholar and philosopher.[24] Similarly, Kasravi's lack of attacks on most of the Iranian intellectual traditions in Ā'in seems to suggest that at the time he was not all that opposed to it, and suggests that his views did not change during these few years. At the same time, the 'old' Kasravi

---

[22] Ahmad Kasravi and Mohammad Amini, *Zendegi va Zamāneh-ye Ahmad-e Kasravi/ Life and Time of Ahmad Kasravi* (Los Angeles: Ketab Corp., 2016), 549–51.
[23] Cf. Ahmad Kasravi, *Khāharān va Dokhtarān-e Mā* ('Our Sisters and Daughters'), n.d., 18–21, and Ahmad Kasravi, 'Mādarān va Khāharān-e Mā, 3' ('Our Mothers and Sisters') *Peymān* 1, no. 3 (1312 (1943)): 21–2.
[24] Ahmad Kasravi, 'Do Ketāb-e Sudmand' ('Two Beneficial Books') in *Kārvand-e Kasravi* ('The Works of Kasravi'), ed. Yahyā Zokā, 2536 (1977–8), 519–20. It was originally published in Armaghān in 1309 (1921).

considered philosophy a waste of time. In his autobiography he expressed satisfaction that as a young man he managed to escape the 'pitfalls of logic' and did not consider philosophy a valid way of spending time (abandoning it after two classes). He admitted, however, that being an inquisitive youth he might have well fallen into these pitfalls.[25]

This change of *Peymān*'s line – the focus on censure of the Iranian intellectual tradition, and especially the gradual move to attack Shiism – led to most of the previous readers abandoning *Peymān* around its fourth year of publication. Those most faithful to Kasravi stayed, and then the new readers flocked.[26] The followers of *Ā'in* left, and the future followers of Pākdini took their place.

Thus, it is fitting to say that while the first years of *Peymān* were the 'era of *Ā'in*', Kasravi later drifted away from the original message of his 'ethos'. After a few years of intellectual development, he would move on to another project, the successor of *Ā'in* – *Varjāvand Bonyād*. It is very telling, however, that even in 1943, when *Bonyād* replaced *Ā'in* and even *Peymān* as the chief work of Kasravi's movement, the people were still asking for *Ā'in* and demanding its reedition, praising it for foreseeing the later developments,[27] probably referring to the rivalry between the Western powers, the ensuring crisis, and the failure to address it which would lead to the next great war, or the Second World War, just as it had been predicted in *Ā'in* (Book 1:8).

This is not surprising. Especially from today's perspective, *Ā'in* may seem more approachable than *Bonyād*. The first, and most obvious, reason is that *Ā'in* has been written in clear Persian prose[28] and *Bonyād* in a rather obscure language, used exclusively by Kasravi's followers. As a result, while *Ā'in* ensured early readership and support for *Peymān*, *Bonyād* relied on journals – such as *Parcham* ('Flag' or 'Standard')[29] – written in a more standard language, to

---

[25] Ahmad Kasravi and Mohammad Amini, *Zendegi va Zamāneh-ye Ahmad-e Kasravi/ Life and Time of Ahmad Kasravi* (Los Angeles: Ketab Corp., 2016), 74–9.
[26] 'Goftār-e Āqā-ye Soltānzādeh,' 22–3.
[27] 'Cherā'.
[28] Although at that time the men of letters would criticize Kasravi's style (Mohammad Qazvini, 'Āzari yā Zabān-e Bāstān-e Āzarbāygān', in *Bist Maqāleh-ye Qazvini*, ed. 'Abbās Eqbāl Āshtiyāni (Tehran: Asātir, 1391), 141–8), *Ā'in*'s language is quite powerful both as a medium of information and logical argument, and as a vehicle of emotions. Had it not been such, neither *Ā'in* nor *Peymān* would have amassed the following and fame they did.
[29] Kasravi published three periodicals titled *Parcham*: a daily newspaper (1942), a bi-weekly (1943) and a weekly (1944).

introduce new followers to Kasravi's ideas.[30] It is also noteworthy that *Ā'in*'s criticism of consumerism and the West's efforts to subjugate the East, while available also in *Bonyād*, became, in the latter work, after the experiences of twentieth-century totalitarianisms and genocides, tainted by calls to kill useless poets and people who spread supposedly harmful teachings,[31] and to force idle people – or people whose work would be considered 'parasitism' – to work in useful professions.[32]

Thus, apart from the inherent value of *Ā'in* as commentary on modernity and expansionism which has managed to stay more relevant than its supposed replacements, the work has an added benefit: it gives the reader the perspective necessary to dispel misconceptions surrounding the life and work of Ahmad Kasravi. Furthermore, the lack of a critical, English edition of this fundamental work certainly contributed to the spread of some of these myths. The available English translations of Kasravi's work, as well as the English-language scholarship on Kasravi, certainly contributed to these misconceptions; if not by the mistakes of the authors, then by the choice of the subject matter.[33] The critical publication of a proper translation of Kasravi's most important non-historical work[34] allows for a more balanced view of the authoritative twentieth-century Iranian scholar, and one of the most important authors who recognized and challenged the Western influence in the East.

---

[30] Explicitly stated in: Ahmad Kasravi, 'Varjāvand Bonyād va Zabān-e Ān' ('*Varjāvand Bonyād* and Its Language'), *Parcham* 1, no. 10 (1943): 400.
[31] Ahmad Kasravi, *Varjāvand Bonyād* (Cologne: Mehr, 1377 (1998–1999)), 150–3.
[32] Ahmad Kasravi, *Varjāvand Bonyād* (Cologne: Mehr, 1377 (1998–1999)), 131–3, 164–7.
[33] See the *A Note on Translation* in the present volume.
[34] It is unclear to what extent the earlier attempt to translate *Ā'in* into English was successful; it had been, however, undertaken by one of his followers: cf. Mahmud Katirā'i, 'Ketābshenāsi', 372.

Index

A

Abbasid Caliphate 162, 162n.32
Academy of Motion Pictures Arts and Sciences (AMPAS) 169n.35
Achaemenids 161, 161n.29
administration, state 157–60, 165
Aesop
  'The North Wind and the Sun' 56–7, 56n.17
agriculture 149–50
Agricultural Adjustment Act (US) 66n.23
Al-e Ahmad, Jalal 2, 15, 54n.14, 187–8, 192
  Dar Khedmat va Khiyānat-e Rowshanfekrān ('The Services and Disservices of the Intellectuals') 187–8
Amini, Mohammad 196
anarchism 37n.9
Andreas, Fredrich Carl 10
animals, comparison to humans 87, 88, 93–4, 106, 113, 115, 141, 185
antithesis 130–1, 130n.16, 158
Arab Bedouins 77, 77n.27
Arabic literature and culture 187
Ashuri, Daryush 15
Āzādegān 190, 190n.13

B

Bagehot, Walter 82n.30
Baha'i 188, 188n.8, 189
Barltold, Vasily 10
Bayat, Morteza Qoli 14
Bazargan, Mahdi 2
beasts, wild. *See* animals
beautification, self- 84, 119, 150
Bedouinism 65, 65n.22, 95
beneficence 79. *See also* good deeds; hospitality
Bible 68n. 164. *See also* Christianity
Bolshevism 41, 41n.10, 127–30, 129n.15, 131, 144, 151

book burnings (*Ketābsuzān*) 186, 186n.1
Britain. *See* United Kingdom
Browne, Edward G. 12
Budapest 50, 78
business. *See* commerce and trade

C

capitalism. *See* commerce and trade; machines
Cassuto, Umberto 68n.
catastrophe (*patiyāreh*) 23n.
Centre for the Dissemination of Islamic Truths (*Kānun-e Nashr-e Haqāyeq-e Eslāmi*) 14
charity. *See* good deeds
chastity 74, 75
China, Sino-Japanese war 111, 111n.6, 120, 126, 168, 179, 180
chivalry (*rādmardi*) 31, 31n.3. *See also* virtue
Christensen, Arthur Emanuel 10
Christianity 40, 116, 167. *See also* Bible
cinema 42, 169, 169n.35
city-dwelling (*shahri-gari*) 63, 63n.20
civilization and civility 63–6, 63n.20, 64n.21, 94–5, 141, 177, 194
clans 63, 111n. 141–2
coexistence, ethos of 133, 134, 135, 141–2, 171, 173, 194–5
colonialism 176–8. *See also* Orientalism
commerce and trade 41–3, 107–8, 119, 124–5, 182–4, 193
competition 84–5, 134, 142, 193
constitutionalism 14
Constitutional Revolution 6–7, 12, 54–5, 54n.15, 157, 157n.28, 159, 162, 165
consumerism. *See* commerce and trade
contentment and tranquility
  agriculture and 149–50
  basis for 134, 171

coexistence, ethos of 133, 134, 135,
    141–2, 171, 173, 194–5
  desire for 21
  vs. happiness 21n.
  historical accounts, importance of
    learning 145
  hospitality 145–8, 148n.27, 149
  vs. machines and modernity 19, 21–2,
    25–7, 29–30, 96, 105, 133
  from religion 91
Crusades 130, 130n.17
Cyrus the Great 161n.29

D

Dadmesteter, James 10
Darwin, Charles 33n.5
Darwinism 110n.4, 114, 114n.7, 115n.8,
    139, 169, 176. *See also* social
    Darwinism
Dashti, Ali 13
deceitfulness. *See* lies and deceitfulness
deeds. *See* good deeds
desert-dwelling (*biyābāni-gari*) 63, 65,
    65n.22
Devotees of Islam (Fadā'iyān-e Eslām) 2,
    187, 188
dishonesty. *See* lies and deceitfulness
dispositions 82–3, 93, 113–14, 133, 134,
    167–70, 171, 173, 185
dominion, over others 127–8
Donyā-ye Islam (journal) 15
Durant, Will
  The Case for India, 195, 195n.20

E

East
  colonial treatment of 176–8
  Europe, relationship with 39, 53, 54,
    57, 61, 138, 159
  historical background 137–8
  hospitality 145–8, 148n.27
  morality and good deeds 53–4, 59–61,
    79, 113–14, 149
  need to refrain from looking towards
    Europe 81–6, 97
  superiority over West 61, 135
  women 71
  See also Europism; Iran; religion
Easternism (*sharqi-gari*) 135, 135n.19

economic inequality. *See* inequality
education 75, 155–6
Eisenhower, Dwight D. 168n.33
employment 46–7, 74. *See also*
    unemployment
Enayat, Hamid 15
equality (fraternity), ethos of 138, 144, 153–4
Estakhri (Abu Ishāq Ibrahim ibn-
    Muhammad al-Farsi) 146, 146n.22
ethics. *See* dispositions; good deeds
eugenics 114, 114n.7, 115, 115n.8
Europe
  agriculture and 149–50
  animals, comparison to 115–16
  animosities within 109–11
  antithesis and 130–1, 158
  approach to 175, 192–3
  civilization, loss of 64–6, 194
  colonialism by 176–8
  commerce and trade 41–3, 107–8, 119,
    124–5, 182–4, 193
  defects and woes 19–20, 39–43, 45,
    66, 95–6, 101, 105–8, 142–4, 172,
    181–2, 185
  East, relationship with 39, 53, 54, 57,
    61, 138, 159
  East, superiority of over 61, 135
  education and 155–6
  European superiority 1, 5, 8, 62
  greed and materialism 49–50, 51–2,
    79–80, 83, 93, 107, 167–70
  inequalities 37–8, 50–1, 50n. 60, 65–6,
    78, 95, 107, 125–6, 149
  irreligiosity 32–4, 33n.4, 39–40, 69–70,
    87, 105–6, 130
  judicial system 162–4
  laws 37–8, 37n.9, 40, 64, 154, 158–9
  liberty and equality 138, 144, 153–4
  need to refrain from looking towards
    81–6, 97
  reason, loss of 110, 110n.4
  religion, need for 113
  sciences and 8–9, 67–70, 134–5
  use of term, 19n.
  war, support for 111–12
  women 71, 73, 74
  See also Europism; machines; social
    Darwinism; United States of
    America

Europism (*urupāgarā'i*)
adoption of European laws 154
appeal of 55–6, 138
critiques of 1, 5–9, 15, 192–3
definition 54n.14
vs. Easternism 135n.19
folly of 61–2, 81, 84–5, 102–3, 145, 181, 184
misguided leaders 77–80, 139–40, 172–3
return to Islam as counter to 13
See also Europe; machines

F
factories. *See* machines
Fadā'iyān-e Eslām (Devotees of Islam) 2, 187, 188
Fardid, Ahmad 2, 15, 54n.14, 192
feudalism 144, 154
fiqh (Islamic jurisprudence) 161–2, 161n.30, 163
First World War (Great War) 21, 21n.1, 41, 41n.11, 110, 181, 193
Foreign Trade Monopoly Bill (Qānun-e Enhesār-e Tejārat-e Khāreji) 81n.
France 66, 66n.24, 78, 106, 116, 130, 154, 162–3
fraternity (equality), ethos of 138, 144, 153–4
Furughi, Muhammad 'Ali 11, 13
futuwwa (youth, manliness) 77n.27

G
Gandhi, Mohandas 120n.10
gender roles. *See* women
Geneva Conventions 110–11, 111n.5, 168, 179–80
gharbzadegi (Westoxication) 54n.14, 192. *See also* Europism
good deeds
for countering misdeeds 125n.
decline of 53–4, 59–60
ethos of 79, 113–14, 149
in Europe 144
vs. greed 169–70
hospitality 145–8, 148n.27
religion and 31–2, 36, 39–40, 88, 90–1
governments
administration and taxation 157–60, 165
constitutionalism 14

dominion over others 127–8
inequalities and 119–20, 182
judicial system 35, 161–5
Great Britain. *See* United Kingdom
Great Depression 9, 60n.18, 66n.23, 118, 118n.9
Great Lockdown 66n.23
Great War (First World War) 21, 21n.1, 41, 41n.11, 110, 181, 193
greed 49, 79–80, 83, 93–4, 106–7, 114, 148, 167–70. *See also* materialism

H
halal 46n.13
Halley Comet 189–90
Hamedan 25, 25n.2
happiness. *See* contentment and tranquility
harām 46n.13
health care 168, 168n.34
Hegel, Georg Wilhelm Friedrich 130n.16
hijab 71n.25
honesty 89, 90
Hoover, Herbert 179n.37
hospitality 145–8, 148n.27. *See also* good deeds
humanism/ethos of humanity (*ādami-gari*)
about 89, 89n.32, 94–5, 135
Europe, loss of 78, 142–4, 180, 181–2
religion and 13, 87–8, 113, 139, 194–5
humankind
coexistence, ethos of 133, 134, 135, 141–2, 171, 173, 194–5
comparison to animals 87, 88, 93–4, 106, 113, 115, 141, 185
competition and 84–5, 134, 142, 193
dispositions 82–3, 93, 113–14, 133, 134, 167–70, 171, 173, 185
distress, causes of 19, 22–3, 89
divine mentors, need for 185
European view of 93
hostilities among 23–4
life, pillars of 133–4, 135, 141, 171, 173
souls 88, 94, 130
See also contentment and tranquility; good deeds; greed; materialism; religion

I

Ibn Battuta 146–7, 146n.24
India 114, 120, 120n.10, 126
inequality, social and economic
  in Europe 37–8, 50–1, 50n.60, 65–6, 78, 95, 107, 125–6
  machines and 40–1, 45–6, 83, 107, 108, 117–19, 129, 150–1
integrity 89, 90
International Monetary Fund 66n.23
inventions. *See* machines
Iran
  Constitutional Revolution 6–7, 12, 54–5, 54n.15, 157, 157n.28, 159, 162, 165
  judicial system 161–2, 165
  Kasravi's influence on 2
  morality and good deeds 53–4, 59–61, 79, 113–14, 149
  post-constitutional intellectual trends 2–4
  taxation and state administration 157–8, 159–60
  See also East; Europism
Iranshahr (journal) 2–3
irreligiosity. *See* religion
Islam 13, 15. *See also* prophets; Quran; religion; Shi'i Islam; Sufism
Islamic jurisprudence (*fiqh*) 161–2, 161n.30, 163
Islamic philosophy 131n.18, 196–7

J

Japan, Sino-Japanese war 111, 111n.6, 120, 126, 168, 179, 180
javānmardi (Knightly Men) 77n.27, 147, 147n.26
jihad 146n.23
judicial system 35, 161–5
Justi, Ferdinand 10

K

Kant, Immanuel 12
Kasravi, Ahmad
  about 1, 186–7, 198
  assassination 2, 14, 187, 188
  attacks against and misconceptions of 13–14, 187–9
  on constitutionalism 14
  Europe and Europism, critiques of 1, 2, 5–9, 192–3, 195–6
  influence of 2, 15
  intellectual influences on 2–4
  Islam and Islamic philosophy 13, 15, 196–7
  Ketābsuzān (book burnings) 186, 186n.1
  legal background 61n.19
  meat and 190, 190n.15
  Orientalism, critiques of 2, 10–12
  Peymān journal 191, 192, 195, 197, 197n.28
  radicalism of 189
  religion and 13, 189–91, 193–5
  vernacular modernity of 2, 15
  on women 71n.25
Kasravi, Ahmad, works
  Ā'in ('Ethos') 5, 191, 192, 195, 196, 197–8, 197n.28, 198n.34
  'East and West' (*Sharq va Gharb*) 10
  Khāharān va Dokhtarān-e Mā ('Our Sisters and Daughters') 71n.25
  Shahryārān-e Gomnām ('Forgotten Rulers') 186
  Tārikh-e Pānsad-Sāleh-ye Khuzestān ('Five-Hundred-Years' History of Khuzestan') 186
  Varjāvand Bonyād ('Sacred Foundation') 189, 192, 197–8
  'What Is Hafiz Saying?' (*Hafez Cheh Miguyad?*) 11
  Zendegāni-ye Man ('My Life') 188–9
Kazemzadeh, Hossein 2, 4, 5, 12, 13
Kermani, Mirza Aqa Khan 12
Ketābsuzān (book burnings) 186, 186n.1
Khomeini, Ruhollah 2, 15, 187
Kipchak 147n.25

L

law
  adoption of European laws 154
  judicial system 35, 161–5
  as pillar of life 133, 134, 171, 173
  religion and 35–8, 40, 64
  taxation and state administration 157–60, 165
leadership 77

League of Nations 21, 21n.1
liberal philosophers 33–4, 33n.5, 69–70, 82, 106, 114–15, 143
liberty, ethos of 138, 144, 153–4
lies and deceitfulness 60–1, 84, 89–90, 94, 96, 169. *See also* greed
life, pillars of 133–4, 135, 141, 171, 173. *See also* coexistence; dispositions; law
literacy 155, 177
London, Bernard 43n.12
London Economic Conference (1933) 179, 179n.37
lordship 127–8

M
Machiavellianism 107, 107n.3, 125, 125n.13, 176
machines
  about 8–9
  abolition, need for 45, 194
  vs. agriculture 149–50
  Bolshevism and 127–9
  vs. civilization 64–5
  commerce and 41–3, 107–8, 119, 124–5, 193
  contentment and tranquility, loss of 21–2, 25–7, 29–30, 96, 105, 133
  deceptiveness of 171–2
  discernment when adopting 134–5, 160, 173
  vs. ethos of humanity 143–4
  harms of 117–20, 134
  inequalities from 40–1, 45–6, 83, 107, 108, 117–19, 129, 150–1
  military technology 6, 23–4, 29, 111–12, 134
  planned obsolescence 42–3, 43n.12, 124–5, 125n.
  self-beautification and 150
  unemployment from 40–1, 120–1, 123–4, 184
Maktab-e Islam (journal) 15
Markwart, Josef 10
marriage 73–4, 75
materialism (*māddigari*) 49–50, 51–2, 83, 193, 195. *See also* greed
Mazdakism 127, 127n.14

medical-industrial complex 168, 168n.34
metaphysical truths 131n.18
military-industrial complex 42, 167–8, 168n.33
military technology 6, 23–4, 29, 111–12, 134
modernity 2, 3, 4, 15
monasteries 147–8, 148n.27
Mongol invasions 137, 137n.20, 147, 162, 162n.32
morality. *See* dispositions; good deeds; greed
Moshfeq Kazemi, Morteza 3
Motahari, Morteza 2

N
Nakhshab, Muhammad 15
Naraqi, Ehsan 15
Negahban, 'Abdollah 191
neoliberalism 106n.2
New Deal 66n.23, 124n.11
Nöldke, Theodore 10
Noqāt al-Kāf, 12
Nuri, Fazl Allah 14

O
obsolescence, planned 42–3, 43n.12, 124–5, 125n.
organs, vestigial 110n.4
Orientalism 2, 10–12, 15, 176, 176n.36. *See also* colonialism

P
Parcham (periodicals) 15, 197, 197n.29
patiyāreh (catastrophe) 23n.
patriotism 78, 109, 112, 182
peace. *See* contentment and tranquility
Peymān (journal) 191, 192, 195, 197, 197n.28
pharmaceutical-industrial complex 168, 168n.34
philosophers, liberal 33–4, 33n.5, 69–70, 82, 106, 114–15, 143
philosophy, Islamic 131n.18, 196–7
planned obsolescence 42–3, 43n.12, 124–5, 125n.
politics 107, 109–10, 125
polygamy 71n.25

progress (*pishraft*) 5–6, 21, 30, 113, 145. *See also* machines
Prohibition 35n.6, 36n.7
prophets
    vs. European philosophers and machines 69–70, 139
    way of life revealed by 49, 51, 64, 79, 90, 113–14, 138, 194
    See also Islam; Quran; religion
Ptolemy 68, 68n.
'Pure Religiosity' (*Pākdini*) 189, 189n.10
Pur-e Reza, Habib Allah 3

Q
Qazvini, Muhammad 3, 12, 197n.28
Quran 33n.4, 111n. 131n.18, 140n.21, 161n.30. *See also* Islam; prophets; religion

R
Rawlinson, George 10
reason 110, 115, 141
religion
    as antidote to world's troubles 31–2, 33–4, 184–5, 193–5
    Asia, origin of 64
    components and pillars of 87–91
    Europe, need for 113
    European irreligiosity 32–4, 33n.4, 39–40, 69–70, 87, 105–6, 130
    foundational role of 68–9, 88
    honesty and 89
    humanism/ethos of humanity and 13, 87–8, 94–5, 96, 113, 139, 194–5
    Kasravi and 13, 189–91, 193–5
    Kazemzadeh on 4
    law and 35–8, 40, 64
    morality and 113–14, 167
    souls 88, 94, 130
    in Soviet Union 129–30, 129n.15, 131
    See also Bible; Christianity; Islam; prophets; Quran
Reza Shah Pahlavi 14, 188, 189, 190
righteousness 79. *See also* good deeds
Roosevelt, Franklin D. 36n.7, 66n.23, 124n.11
Ruhi, Ahmad 12
Rushdie, Salman 187
Russia. *See* Bolshevism

S
Sa'di 11, 37n.8
Sadra, Molla 196
Sa'edi, Gholamreza 2, 15
Safavi, Navvab 188
Safavi, Rahimzadeh 15
Said, Edward 12
Sanā'i Ghaznavi 101n.1
scepticism 113
sciences 8–9, 67–70, 134–5
Second World War 41, 41n.11, 197
Seddiq, Isa 11
self-beautification 84, 119, 150
Shadman, Fakhroddin 2, 15
Shafaq, Rezazadeh 3, 15
Shahabpur, 'Ata Allah 2
Shahidi, Ja'far 2, 15
Shari'ati, Ali 2, 15
Shari'ati, Muhammad Taqi 14, 15
Sheykh va Shukh ('The Cleric and the Jester') 192–3
Shi'i Islam 14, 15, 187, 197
Shiraz 84, 84n.31
Shushtar 84, 84n.31
Sino-Japanese war 111, 111n.6, 120, 126, 168, 179, 180
slave trade 154
social Darwinism 78, 78n.28, 82, 82n.30, 106–7, 106n.2, 114–15, 114n.7, 193, 194. *See also* Darwinism
social inequality. *See* inequality
socialism 37n.9, 65, 78, 96
Sogdia (Sogdiana) 146, 146n.22
souls 88, 94, 130
sovereignty 14
Soviet Union. *See* Bolshevism
Spencer, Herbert 82n.30, 106n.2
state administration 157–60, 165
Steinbeck, John
    The Grapes of Wrath, 60n.18, 66n.23
Sufism 15, 142, 147, 186
Sumner, William Graham 82n.30

T
Taleqani, Mahmud 2
Taqizadeh, Seyed Hasan 7, 12, 55n.16, 79n.29

taxation 157–8, 159
technology. *See* machines
Tehran 25, 25n.2, 84
theft 93. *See also* judicial system; lies and deceitfulness
trade. *See* commerce and trade
tranquillità. *See* contentment and tranquility
Tuti Maraghehi, Mirza Hossein 3

U
unemployment 40–1, 46, 112, 120–1, 123–4, 125, 184
United Kingdom 12, 78, 114, 120n.10
United States of America 35–6, 51, 66n.23, 78, 124, 124n.11, 182–3, 191. *See also* Europe; Europism

V
vestigial organs 110n.4
virtue (*sherāfat*) 31, 31n.3, 36

W
war
  Geneva Conventions and 110–11, 111n.5, 168, 179–80
  military-industrial complex 42, 167–8, 168n.33
  military technology 6, 23–4, 29, 111–12, 134
  Quran on preventing 111n.
waywardness 72
West. *See* Europe; United States of America
Westoxication (*gharbzadegi*) 54n.14, 192. *See also* Europism
women 71–5, 71n.25, 156, 196
world 19, 31. *See also* humankind; religion
World War I. *See* First World War
World War II. *See* Second World War

Z
Zanjān (Zangān) 84, 84n.31
Zāvieh Kord 148n.27

www.ingramcontent.com/pod-product-compliance
Lightning Source LLC
Chambersburg PA
CBHW052112300426
44116CB00010B/1643